# Health for Hooligans

# HEALTH FOR HOOLIGANS

**Sandy Fawkes**

with illustrations by
**Willie Rushton**

**John Pascoe** London

First published as a PPB Original by
John Pascoe Limited, 1982



Set in Century Schoolbook by
Bell AP and Span Graphics
Printed and bound in England by
William Clowes (Beccles) Limited
for the publishers
John Pascoe Limited
45 Old Bond Street
London W1X 3AF

ISBN 0 946359 00 8

## Sandy Fawkes

Sandy Fawkes' education began at 16 when she went to Art School. It progressed through the jazz fraternity by way of marriage, on to television as a researcher, and to graduation in Fleet Street — as good a place as any to take a doctorate in Hooliganism. On a more serious note, she has been Fashion Editor of the *Daily Mail* and chief woman reporter of the *Daily Express* — a job that involved, amongst many major assignments, covering the conflicts in Israel (1973) and Northern Ireland. She is also the author of *Killing Time*, *In Praise of Younger Men* and of a forthcoming book with Christine Keeler.

# FRIENDLY SPIRITS

I would like to raise a glass in thanks to all my friends for their aid and assistance over the years. From the hours spent with them, the need for this book grew! I would also like to thank Helen Hodge of *Healthy Living* magazine, Bernard Linker of Dietary Specialists Limited, and Doctor Len Mervyn of Booker Health Foods Limited for their enthusiastic support for the project, their generous advice, and for opening my eyes to the fact that health experts like a drink too. My thanks, too, to Charles Vetter of ACCEPT for sparing me time to discuss the hazards of unhealthy boozing with good sense and humour. And a general round of thanks to all the healthfood addicts and store owners, who take such care to ensure our life-support ingredients are available. The biggest toast goes to my Superhooligans, who found time in their busy lives to contribute their own hilarious experiences with the Friendly Spirits.

Sandy Fawkes
London, October 1982

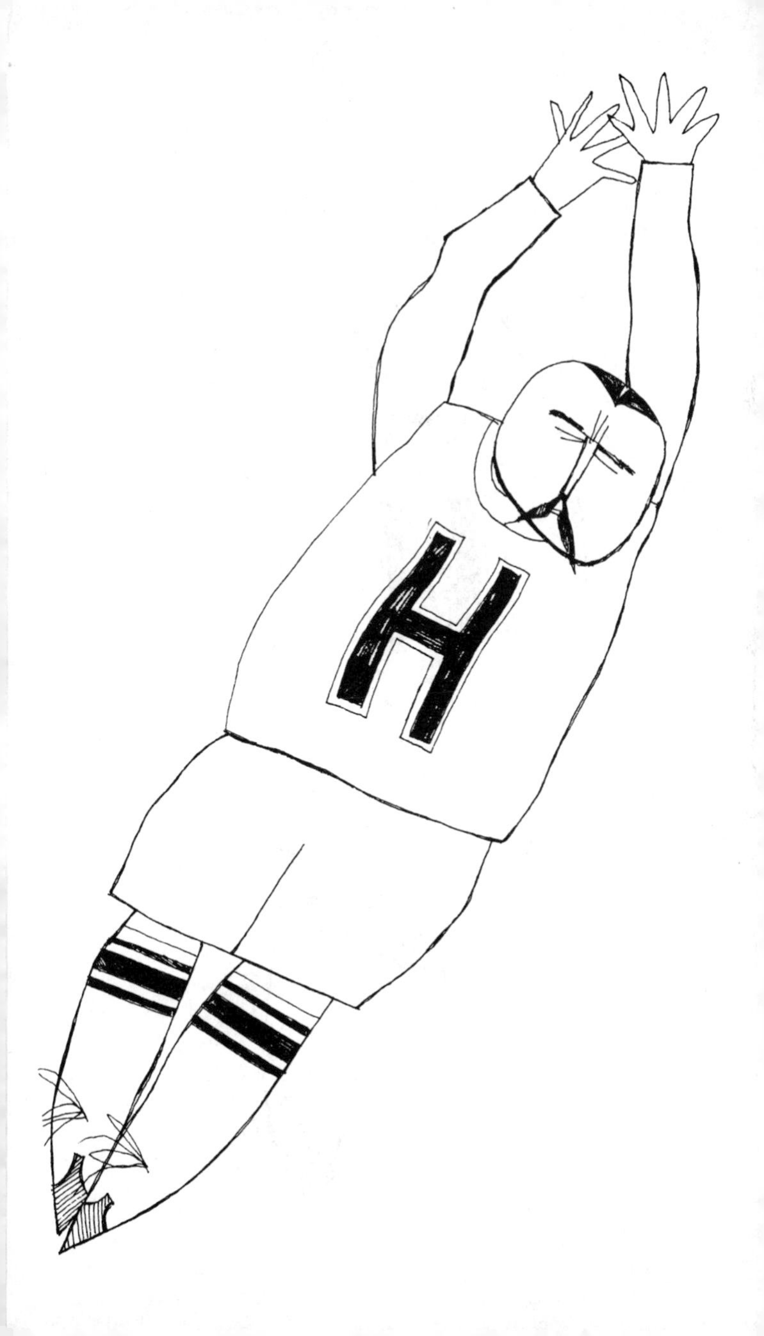

# DEARLY BELOVED . . .

# DEARLY BELOVED . . .

My dictionary describes the word hooligan as 'a member of a street gang', an uncharitable definition to my mind. I think of Hooligans as persons whose entry into a room causes other people's faces to light up with anticipated pleasure. The possibility of mischief has arrived. Alternatively, other people's faces take one look, gulp their drinks at speed, make their excuses and leave. They do not want to be in the sight-lines when the Hooligan turns snappish.

A Healthy Hooligan is a joy to meet — expansive, funny and generous. An Unhealthy Hooligan is a bloody nuisance — belligerent, morose and embarrassing to self and others.

This book is for those of us for whom it is the road *from* Hell that is paved with Good Intentions; for those to whom every Saturday or Monday morning is either Ash Wednesday or New Year's Day, Must-Give-It-Up or Turn-Over-a-New-Leaf. This is not a book for serious health freaks, nor indeed for anyone with a serious turn of mind. It is a handbook for the Haphazard Life.

Hooligans usually drink — there is no denying it. And drink, as any of us who have regarded the crimson veins and bloodshot eye staring balefully back from the morning mirror most surely know, does take rather more toll from the body mechanism than the well controlled From-Mortgage- to-Mortuary lifestyle.

Falter Ye Not at this moment; this is a book of Do not Don't. I would not dream of suggesting that we deprive the Chancellor of the Exchequer of his millions, nor that the ranks of the dole queues should be swelled by adding publicans to it; such irresponsibility would be shocking. I happen to think that we Hooligans are important enough to the world to look after ourselves. We must keep fit in order to create happy havoc yet another day.

So I have sought advice and recipes for those days of Remorse and Resolution, the days that start with anvils ringing and demons singing, from The Experts — from doctors, because they are well-known to be near the top of the drinking league — from healthfood professionals because they have an unconventional outlook on life, and from Superhooligans because they survive a life that involves working as hard as they play. And that in itself is no mean feat.

I have found an abundance of vital information *en route*, and if at any moment I felt threatened with hypochondria I reached for a sensible-sized scotch just to keep the theories straight. Even so, I have to admit to taking the advice herein proffered, and at the conclusion of this research I am a fitter, wiser and jollier Fawkes. I hope you will benefit too.

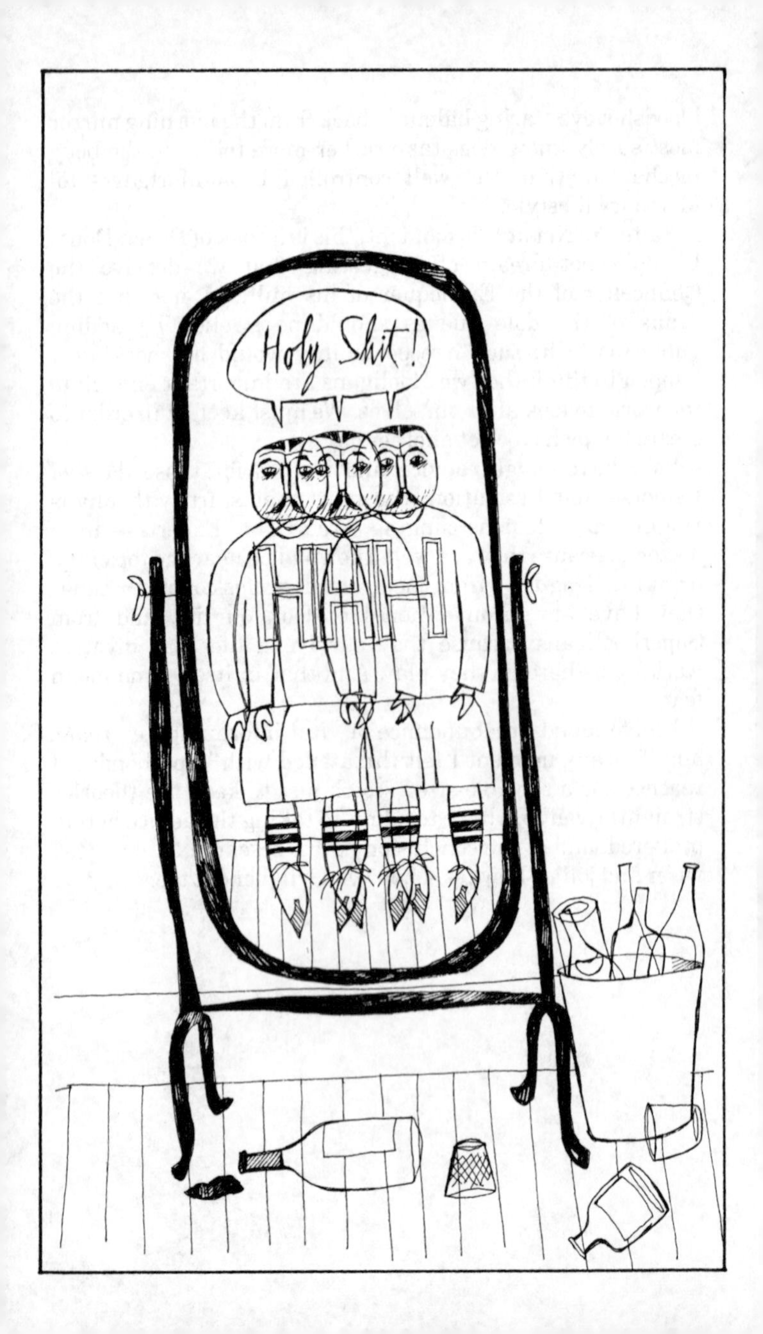
Holy Shit!

# GUARDIAN ANGELS

# GUARDIAN ANGELS

We all know the effect of alcohol. It starts off making you feel relaxed, cheerful, even optimistic, a state that seems well worth sustaining and, more to the point, worth sharing with a few friends. They too become imbued with the goodness of life. It would be churlish to deprive them of such warmth just because you are feeling a bit peckish — so you have another one or seven. And then, to your utter surprise, you are pissed.

If your liver could speak only half as eloquently as you think you have been doing all night it would inform you very tartly that, while it can work as efficiently as Spaghetti Junction, in order to do so properly it needs just that — spaghetti, fish-and-chips, Chinese-take-away, anything. Grub, in other words. The liver is designed for a great diversity of functions, including processing food for the benefit of its owner; if required to deal solely with alcohol it will begin to develop the well-known factory-assembly-line syndrome — and start behaving like a zombie. And a bored liver will sulk.

Just as you may go home and have a row with the wife, lover, or taxi-driver, your liver will fall out in no uncertain terms with its own familiars — your stomach, heart, head and any other bits of your body within snarling distance.

When you try to say you are sorry in the morning it will not be amused. Nor will it be listening, for the simple reason that it will still be hard at work on last night's booze.

If you are feeling really contrite (in other words you have got the most godawful hangover) you will probably try and get back in its good graces by shovelling a good old fry-up down your gullet. Now, according to whether your body is in a benign or a baleful mood, either this treatment will put you on your feet or your head over the lavatory basin. It ain't going to make you a match for Tarzan!

It's odd, really, when you come to think of it; nobody would expect a car to run on fuel alone — getting tanked up is only part of the maintenance. Everyone knows that cars need lubricating, recharging and other predictable attentions. Perhaps it's just because cars cost so much that owners don't abuse them. Our bodies are free. Unfortunately our bodies can't be traded in for new models. Wives can, lovers can, bosses can, but your own private piece of mechanism is all you've got.

So in order to continue enjoying life in this unique machine it is neccessary to learn a bit about body maintenance. Not a lot, just enough to keep Body and Soul together. My reaearch has failed to reveal a guarantee of a Great Big Bar up in the Sky so it's best to make sure you can enjoy the ones down here. We all know we need to eat to live; we also all recognise that alcohol, after a certain point, suppresses the appetite. Now, I don't know if you are as bad as me, but if I've got only a couple of quid in my pocket it is more likely to find its way across the bar of my local than end up in the grocer's till. Shocking but true. *My* excuse is that there is not a lot of fun to be found in a can of baked beans, what's yours? Yes, I know. A large one.

But seriously, as they say, nobody can deny that there are Absolutely Dread Days when Remorse and Retribution are your only companions, and you have to face the fact that Something Must Be Done.

But 'What?' is the pathetic cry . . .

Personally I hide, and it was in one of these states of hibernation that the idea for this book came to me. My body was scolding me like a fishwife and using the same language; it soon became obvious that whichever brain cells I had damaged they were not the ones I would have selected; I could remember my less-than-perfect behaviour all too well. In my case Pride came after the Fall. I realised I hadn't eaten anything more than a couple of sandwiches for days and that I looked bloody awful. I knew that, for once, every hair off a pack of dogs would do me no good whatsoever. It was time for Rest and Recuperation.

I crept round to my local healthfood store in the saintly hope that anything marked 'wholefood' would restore me. I found a confusing array of pills and packages, recalled hearing that vitamin B12 is supposed to be good for bodies, bought the cheapest amount (cunningly keeping enough money lest I should feel strong enough to take a drink later, tut, tut) and picked up a health magazine for good measure — on the principle that having something to read makes you less lonely, so less tempted out to find company.

I skipped briskly past the feature called 'Helping the Speechless' (it is, alas, not one of my shortcomings), and turned my attention to a picture of an array of glasses under the headline 'Top Up with Vitamin C'. The glasses were demonstrably not filled with orange juice but with wine, beer and spirits. Could that possibly mean that healthfood experts didn't only *not* despise the frail and wicked imbiber but could actually help?

The answer was yes, yes, and yes.

**Good news**

Everything from Brewers' Droop to Boozers' Gloom can be tackled with vitamins, as can pre-menstrual tension (which often leads women to get aggressively paralytic drunk), alcoholic insomnia, bruises, bloodshot eyes and bad breath, jet-lag and that universal *bête-noire*, the hangover.

Needless to say, I tackled the hangover first and during my enquiries I discovered a lot of information about the various vitamins we can take to avoid too many morning-after situations as well.

The healthfood writers, producers and suppliers have been most helpful; and before cynics chorus 'well they would, wouldn't they? It helps their sales' let us quietly consider whether anyone has ever raised a similar moral objection to the distillers' and brewers' advertisements. Let's clear the air of another objection frequently raised — that a lot of the supplementary vitamins intake is excreted by the body, proving that they are a waste of money.

So what do you think that frothy morning urine contains? Alcohol, m'dear, and a lot more costly it was to put in.

So here is a brief and cheerful guide to vitamins in what I consider to be the order of importance to Hooligans. I am not detailing minerals because few people seem sufficiently certain about all of them and in any case I am sure their complexities would bore you; but I will include them when they are mentioned for specific cures. Should this book turn you into a Health Hooligan, there are plenty of reference books available for your studies.

**Vitamin C**

The first thing to know about vitamin C is that the body needs to be fed it every single day. It can be found in oranges, lemons and grapefruit, also in tomatoes, cabbage, green peppers and potatoes. Most doctors claim that one orange a day will provide an adequate intake for the average person's needs. But a Hooligan is *not* your average person; he is inclined to do everything to excess. I firmly believe that Hooligans will be happier adopting the same attitude towards their vitamins.

Helen Hodge, the editor of *Healthy Living*, stated categorically that the serious drinker could drown in orange juice before it would provide the amount of vitamin C needed to combat an evening out on the troll. She advises taking megadoses of the stuff before, during and after drinking.

Now that is not half as difficult as it sounds at first, because vitamin C comes in effervescent one-gram tablets as well as conventional tablets of lower dosage, all of which can be bought at any chemist's. And one gram is a mammoth amount when compared to a measly 30 milligrams, the minimal daily rate officially recommended for health.

The advice to take vitamin C during drinking is logical in that alcohol depletes the body's supply plus the fact that vitamin C passes through the body in three to four hours. But I have to admit that it is not very practical for a night out on the town. The very request for a simple glass of water in the middle of a session would put your mates in a state of culture shock; solemnly to dissolve a large white tablet before their very eyes would surely guarantee a chill in the proceedings, a sort of unspoken recognition that the phrase 'what's your poison?' isn't so far off the mark. Better to take two when you get home — though if it has been the kind of evening that results in your waking fully clothed at two in the morning, dehydrated and dying for a piddle, that is as good a time to take them as any. When you stagger back to bed (undress as they dissolve), your friendly vitamin C will diligently saturate your tissues, gathering up the toxics ready for a

Dunkirk-style exit in the morning.

Daily drinkers will not need to be told to re-equip the body for the invasion on the morrow, so they should acquire the habit of taking one every morning. It is also sensible to keep a supply in the office desk to take before or after a lunchtime session.

Vitamin C is a mild diuretic, so your visits to the loo may be more frequent if you have nothing in your stomach to delay its journey.

Differing lifestyles need different quantities daily, and since there are no proven toxic effects you cannot overdose on vitamin C. Doses of vitamin C are measured in grams and milligrams (no, I didn't know that 1000 mg make 1 gram either).

For instance, each cigarette smoked destroys about 25 mg so the smoker should multiply the number of cigarettes per day by 25 and take the result in milligrams on top of the total of vitamin C for all their other iniquities. Bearing in mind the speedy rate of exit of the vitamin, it is better to take, say, 200 mg tablets three times a day. Since an orange contains a mere 25-30 mg, you can see the impossibility of combatting the depletion naturally. Carbon monoxide destroys vitamin C, so do anxiety situations, the taking of aspirin and the Pill, not forgetting our old friend alcohol. Taking it regularly helps prevent colds (it is recommended to attack the first signs of one by taking a gram every hour until all symptons dissappear), helps diminish blood cholesterol, and aids the healing of wounds — a piece of information for which the Unhealthy Hooligan should be exceptionally grateful.

Altogether vitamin C turns out to be a cheery little life and energy restorer aimed at putting you back on the path to health as quickly as possible.

There are many symptons of vitamin C deficiency long before we reach the scurvy stage; chronic fatigue, that feeling that life is hardly worth living, is one of them. The awful thing is that when you need your vitamins most is when you feel least like making the effort to take them. A very understandable situation, this; but you have to start somewhere and vitamin C shows the quickest results. Other indications that you are running your body on short supply are recurring outbreaks of spots, scratches and cuts that don't heal, an easily upset stomach and a tendency to bruise at the slightest knock.

Vitamin C, known chemically as ascorbic acid, is available at most chemists in a variety of forms. It is recommended by The Experts that if you are going to go for the megadoses (and, after all, Hooligans never do anything by halves) you could be better off taking the organic forms that come from rose hip, also you could look out for the kind bonded with calcium. Best thing to do is to ask at your local healthfood store, and if that seems too much of a chore, just pop into your local Boots where their own brand is very cheap.

Working it out roughly, the price of counteracting the effect of smoking 20 cigarettes a day is half that of a single fag, so maintaining some sort of body balance costs about the price of one packet of cigarettes a month. The hefty boozer on three grams of effervescent vitamin C per day spends slightly less than the price of a bottle of tonic a day on keeping fitter.

**The Vitamins B**

A complicated little lot, these, but the only ones we need to know about are B1, B2, B6, and B12. Once again the body needs them daily; and they can be found in brewers' yeast, whole-grain cereals, liver, fish, nuts, potatoes, milk, cheese, mushrooms, cabbage and eggs. Not all of them are found in each food, but a well-balanced diet would provide them all. Which brings us to the rub and the need for the vitamins B in supplementary form because, inevitably, they succumb to alcohol and smoking.

The Bs are called the anti-stress vitamins for the simple reason that a shortage of them makes you irritable, twitchy and lethargic. These are definitely the vitamins to reach for when you feel tempted to tell the boss where to shove his job, when a ring on the doorbell makes you jump out of your skin because it is more likely to be the bailiff than a long-lost wealthy friend, or when you are so depressed that a shave before going to the local is just too much effort.

At these low moments you will not be in the mood to wonder which particular dosages you need, so the sensible thing is to grasp whichever high-potency vitamin B complex is handiest and take it from there.

Having gained some semblance of equilibrium (they do give quite a cheering lift) you can proceed to study your needs.

Since it is unlikely that you are suffering from beriberi, I'll just tell you that vitamins B1 and B2 are the ones known to improve morale; they are also the ones that have been grabbed by all the nicotine and alcohol so you need a plentiful supply of them for yourself because they look after your nervous system, heart and muscles. Your hand will probably be shaking as you raise the glass of water to your mouth.

Vitamin B6 is particularly good for women, both those on the Pill and those who suffer pre-menstrual tension, because it is a natural diuretic and drains from the body the excess fluid that causes that depressing fat feeling. Dosage should be

discussed with your local healthfood store owner.

Vitamin B12, the Sozzlers' Saviour, is better absorbed when taken with vitamin B6. It is the great revitaliser and helps improve concentration — very useful to both the executive class after an expense-account lunch and the skilled craftsman who has spent his hour off at the local. It is also said to improve the memory but you may not wish to know that.

All these vitamins do have other functions like looking after the red blood cells and the tissues that produce antibodies; but I don't think that's the info you are seeking here — it was just a bonus thought. Doses are given in milligrams (mg), and are best taken in high-potency, slow-release form, preferably after breakfast. If you take them without food they won't do you any harm, but they can repeat on you with a sort of yeasty taste.

For the days when you have a hundred and one things to do and don't know where to start, vitamin B6 plus Chamomile gives you energy and has a calming effect at the same time — truly a panic-over tablet, also good for the racing brain if you can't get to sleep.

Try not to economise on buying vitamins B unless you are already enjoying a fairly wholesome diet. Always look at the label to see how many tablets you should take a day, and do a bit of mental arithmetic. I think you will find a month's supply even of the megadosage forms will cost you less than a daily paper for the same period. The prices and quantities of B vitamins included do vary with each make, but those short of cash will find brewers' yeast tablets very reasonable; you just need to take them more often. Many people prefer them because they are the purest source of the whole B complex.

Vitamin B6 plus Chamomile comes in capsule form, and costs less per day than the copper coins you wouldn't bother to pick up from the floor.

**Vitamin E**

This one is known as the rejuvenating vitamin. It is stored in the liver, heart, muscles and your loving glands, so ought to be essential for anyone secretly nurturing a suspicion that they are getting too old for sex. Also, because it regenerates the tissues it is good for the skin, and helps to keep the muscles in healthy working order. It can be absorbed through the skin, and so is very useful in healing wounds and burns (flagellists and masochists please note). It can be found in wheat germ, vegetable oils, greens including brussel sprouts and spinach (that's what Popeye was on about — no wonder his lady was called Olive Oil), whole grain cereals and eggs.

Wheatgerm capsules can be bought at Boots or healthfood stores, where you can also buy tablets of vitamins E plus C for instant vitality. These are chewable, so extra useful for anyone doubting their ability to fulfil their obligations.

It is measured in International Units (IU); 400 IU is a reasonable amount to take, but if looking for miracles try increasing the dosage.

Vitamin E is also recommended for women during the menopause. Vitamin E creams, lotions, shampoos and soap are available at healthfood stores, and at Boots in their 'Original Formula' and 'Number Seven' ranges.

Vitamin E is packaged in many combinations and strengths, but the absolutely top-whack price works out at around the cost of your tabloid newspaper per day, and will almost certainly make you feel a lot better.

**Vitamin A**

Yet another Hooligans' friend, this one, as it affects the eyes, hearing, senses of smell and taste, and the lungs — all of which are liable to come under strain as we cavort from work under artificial light to smoke-filled pub, on to darkened noise-filled disco and so on. It is comforting to know that it is not our life-style that leaves us utterly exhausted but our lack of Vitamin A.

This one is stored in the body — in the liver, in fact — and we can expect to find enough of this vitamin in our everyday food. Anyone with a severe eye infection will need extra; so will those with chronic night blindness (I'm afraid not being able to see across a nightclub or having to grope your way up the stairs does not count), who may already have symptons of shortage.

Vitamin A is found in carrots, margarine, watercress (so eat up your garnish even if it is considered bad manners), eggs, milk, liver, cod-liver oil and fish roe.

If you are worried about your eyesight going (first sign being that you think you need longer arms to read the newspaper) or that you might be going a bit mutton-jeff, you could try cod-liver oil capsules for a while.

Now Vitamin A is one of the few vitamins it *is* possible to overdose on; the advice from The Experts is to take it five days on the trot, then leave it out for two. It is measured in IU, and the body needs about 5000 IU daily; but once again, always ask at your local healthfood store if you think you need more.

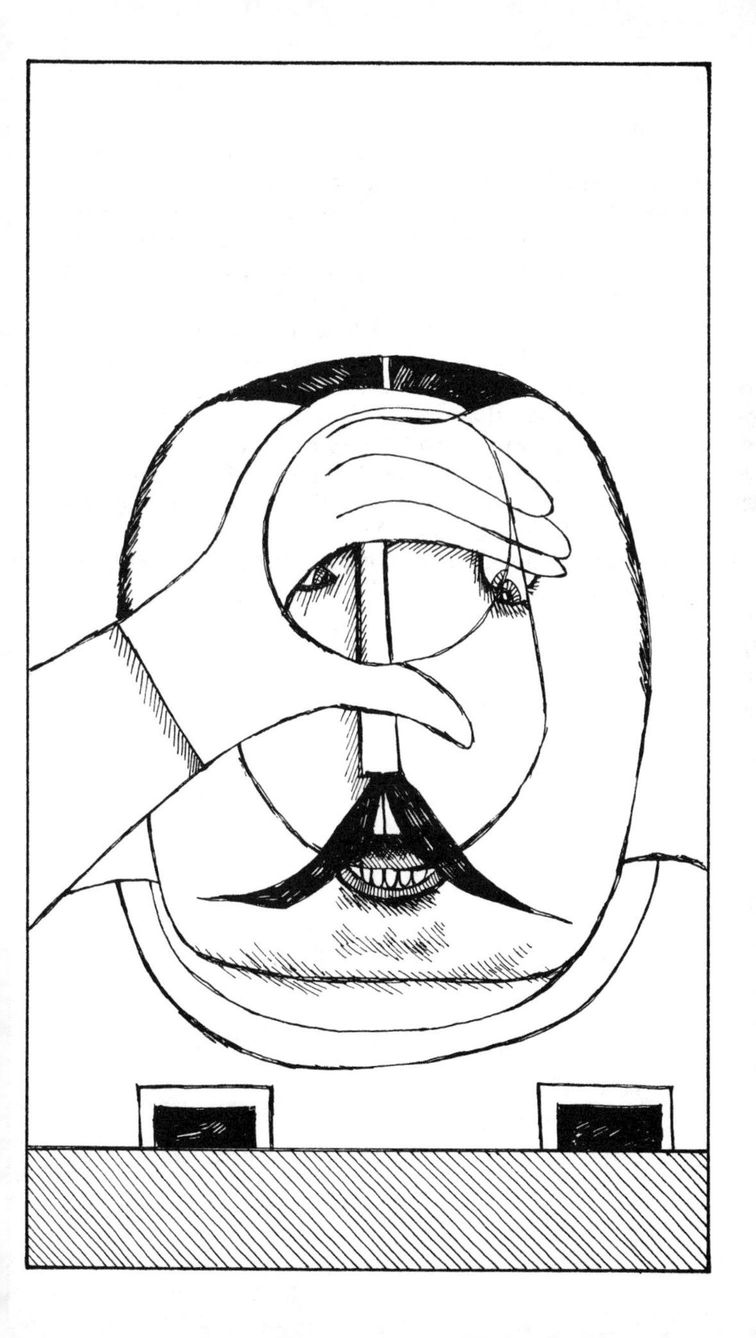

**Vitamin D**
Also known as the 'Sunshine Vitamin' for the simple reason that the ultraviolet rays of the sun act on the oils of the skin to manufacture the vitamin, which is then absorbed into the body. But because the body stops producing vitamin D as soon as your suntan is established, you can have a wonderfully healthy-looking tan and still catch a cold.

You can make up for this deficiency by sitting in the shade eating fresh sardines, tuna fish salad, herrings, salmon or caviar. On the other hand you could take your cod-liver oil capsules and know that they are working with the vitamin A to make sure your teeth don't fall into your glass.

If you are a night-worker (or player) or prefer to spend your lunchtime in some hostelry rather than sit on a park bench, you will need extra vitamin D in order to avoid rickets and the dentist's drill, but do look at the label and take only the recommended dose.

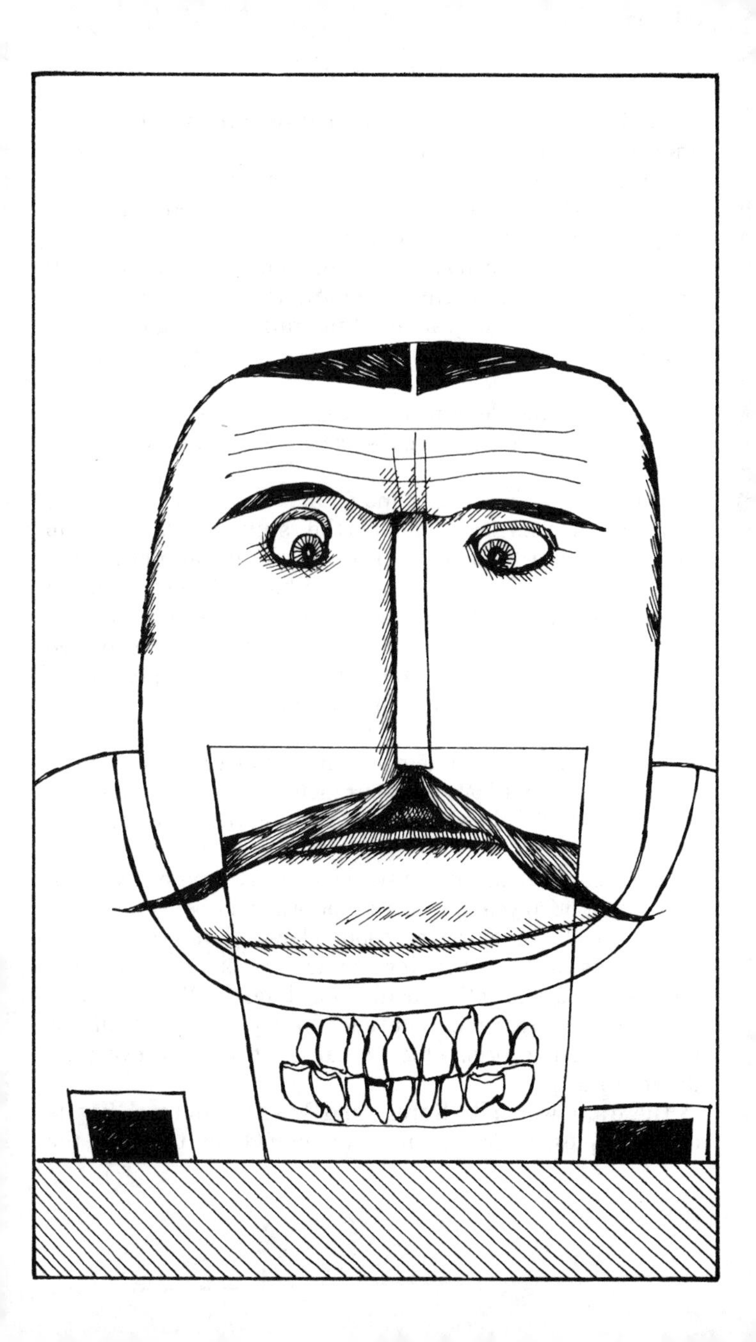

Should you have it in mind to disregard all the above information, let me implore you, please try to take at least one multivitamin per day; you'd be daft not to, and if you really have been letting yourself go, not eating etcetera, take two — one in the morning and one at night.

Go for the healthfood manufacturers if you get a choice; all the vitamins and minerals are guaranteed organic and more easily absorbed. But grab anything rather than go without. One capsule of health will set you back the price of a box of matches.

Should you decide that there just might be such a thing as Health for Hooligans, I've got some more good news.

*Garlic perles* have been around for ages — at least as long as werewolves who can't abide the stuff. In addition to protecting us from mythological beasts (though not neccessarily pink ones), garlic is the great blood cleanser, and the perles are concentrated garlic. Three taken at night (in cold water as they are encased in gelatin) will keep you bright-eyed and bushy-tailed by the simple process of gathering up the garbage in your blood, including excess cholesterol.

Garlic perles do not make you smell like a French railway porter, but they will prevent your mouth tasting and smelling like the proverbially ethnic-owned armpit the following day.

*Ginseng* has been around even longer; the Chinese have been using it for 5000 years. It has a reputation for being mentally and physically invigorating, though how it does so is about as mysterious as the country it comes from. It is supposed to be a panacea, a cure for all your ills — a claim the Western mind is inclined to treat with caution. Taking ginseng should be treated with caution too, because it affects everyone differently.

There are two kinds, Korean and Siberian, and each has its own disciples. To try it out, take one 600 mg tablet in the morning before eating. It isn't sensible to take it before you go out on a bender because you risk getting as high as a kite. Taken early, it has had time to be assimilated into the system before you introduce it to your favourite tipple.

It needs to be taken regularly in order to build up its (and your) full potency, so if you feel a bit odd at first, keep on trying and see if you feel better after a week or ten days. It is sometimes coyly referred to as the 'man-like' herb because it is shaped like a big dick — which may well be why it is revered as a cure for impotence out East. There are times when anything is worth a try.

*Zinc* is a mineral, one of the things I said I wouldn't bother you with; but this one is important as it is essential to your well-being and — you've guessed it — gets washed out by alcohol. If you are lacking in zinc the alcohol stays in the body longer, and the danger of build-up is higher. The consequence is that a few drinks at lunchtime will make you drunk very quickly, an event that could cause bosses to reach for your personal file and friends to remember other appointments. Basically you are on your way to alcoholic poisoning. A high-protein meal is the answer — steak, liver, fish — though once again I recognise that this advice is impractical on the occasion you are caught out. The quickest form of rescue is 10–20 mg of chelated zinc plus vitamins B and C, and a promise not to let it happen again.

# The Morning After.

# PURGATORY AND PENANCE

# PURGATORY AND PENANCE

A little knowledge is not necessarily such a bad thing; I, personally have no wish for too much inside information. The surgeon who told a friend of mine that if his (the friend's) liver had been served to him in a restaurant he would have sent it back was being over-diligent, to my mind.

Which is another way of saying that, logically, we can help ourselves over the smaller hurdles of life with the sensible application of vitamins to the mouth — though real troubles do call for medical help or professional aid.

Vitamins will help restore many a precarious body balance. In some cases (with expert advice) they can be used to cure certain illnesses, but that is beyond the scope of this book. I would also like to point out that it is beyond the scope of the lone vitamin to cope with a whole bottle of the hard stuff; I know all about David and Goliath, but they were playing a different ball game.

Below is a list of vitamin combinations and medicaments likely to be needed by Hooligans for Operations Rescue.

**Hangovers**
Oystertone was one of the more amazing of my discoveries during research for this book. It comes in capsule form, and each one contains the essence of approximately seven Pacific oysters.

Now oysters have long been known for their restorative values — by playboys and mother's-ruin consumers alike. A dozen to settle the stomach, whether *en route* to the Ritz or the nearest gin-palace, was commonplace when the delicious little objects were cheap. The late Bernard Walsh built his Wheeler's empire on them. Sadly, oysters are now a luxury, and only the rich can afford to be healthy. Or so I thought. But luckily the Japanese have spent 25 years turning them into this very democratic product that can be bought over the counter of independent chemists and healthfood stores.

Admittedly the Japanese had slightly higher ideals than rescuing us from our agonies as they laboured over their researches; the oyster pill is aimed at relieving heart problems, helping diabetics and those suffering from rheumatism or arthritis.

It just so happens that they contain, in instantly absorbable form, all the minerals and vitamins that a night on the sauce has removed from the body.

It is claimed that one taken before drinking enables its recipient to continue drinking much longer; this piece of information could be dangerous for the heavy consumer in that it may give him freedom to feel doubly reckless. Quite frankly, when I investigated this claim I felt as daft as a brush within the hour; so if you want to feel as silly as you were ten years ago, it's up to you.

However, they are absolutely superb if taken last thing at night. All those busy minerals and vitamins do their job valiantly, and you wake up feeling bright and clean. For the forgetful, one taken first thing in the morning clears the head sufficiently to make your colleagues' day unbearable. Ray MaCabe, the landlord of the Golden Lion in Soho, tried them out and found himself shifting 70 kegs of beer before breakfast.

Not to go too heavy on the point, I think they are so good for you they are worth taking all the time; you don't have to take a drink to get the benefit. Such wellbeing costs less than any bus fare, and you can save that with an energetic walk. Every time you take an expensive and desperate taxi to work you will be spending about the cost of a month's supply of health.

**Home-made cures**

However throbbing the head, try to resist any form of aspirin or caffeine. These, too, rob the body of its recovery larder. Feed it some nourishment instead.

Effervescent vitamin C plus a couple of spoonsful of Fructose (diabetic sugar) can be managed almost with the eyes shut. If the sound of all those jolly bubbles bursting is too much, lean against the closed door while the activity takes place.

A tablespoonful of powdered yeast in a glassful of grapefruit juice (taken in one gulp as in Underberg) will remind you that there is a brain in there somewhere.

Plain yoghurt, a banana, peeled (sorry about the effort), a whole egg, broken (ditto) and a tablespoon of honey, all popped into the liquidiser, is excellent for those suffering from the Puritan Ethic. The noise of the liquidiser is crucifying and would inspire Bertie Wooster to fire Jeeves.

Pampered persons preparing for an expense-account lunch can take their yeast in half a pint of Guinness, thus keeping fit and wagging the tail of the dog. They can even liven it up with a glass of champagne. They'll probably drink the champagne anyway — it is the most marvellous way to turn a hangover day into a flyover day.

**Boozer's gloom**

For anyone agonising their way through the 'I'm Only Fit For The Human Scrapheap' syndrome, I have words of comfort.

It may not have been your fault. Perhaps they were pissed too. Maybe they won't remember.

You've got to start somewhere, and burying your head under the pillow will not make the world go away.

Take a double dose of vitamin B complex. Do not look in the mirror. Go back to bed for half an hour.

The Bells will stop tolling; the boss's wife might have enjoyed you groping her bum; the cheque might not bounce; that gorgeous blonde might even now be wondering what to wear for your lunch date.

Take an effervescent vitamin C and use it to wash down a vitamin E and zinc combine. Some things even vitamins can't cure — telling a lover they are rotten in bed, the landlord of your local that he is a creep, your best friend that you have had it off with his/her partner.

Suggestions; take 600 mg of ginseng. You have now cared for your nerves, your brain and your hopes. Obey the usual ablutions, and hope for inspiration in the form of an imaginative apology. If nothing doing, either sign the pledge or take your drinking habits off the manor for a few days.

**Brewers' droop**

With a friend like him, who needs enemies? It may be all in the mind, as they say, but when a man can't to do what he oughtta do, let alone what he wants to do, things is getting kinda dubious round here.

Now the occasional failure, due to too much time spent in the pub or club a-wooing, can be socially embarrassing, but is not too serious unless she either has to, or chooses to, get up and go home.

The 'Catch-22' situation arises when a man starts drowning his fears of inadequecy night after night, for the very alcohol he is consuming to forget his troubles is actually washing away the vitamins and minerals that would solve his problem. This is where that vitamin E and that mineral zinc can be mighty helpful, because they are both devoted to keeping the sex glands in firm working order.

Embark on a course of Vitamin E in supplement form; there are lots in the healthfood stores, particularly the modern self-service kind. Vitamin E is non-toxic, so can be taken in doses from 400 IU to 1000 IU without harm. It is sensible to build up to a higher dosage over a few weeks to restore the body's confidence. If you can't wait that long, cut down on the booze and take a marvellous combination of vitamin E, ginseng, zinc and a herb called turnera. The Latin name for the last ingredient is *Damiane aphrodisica* (which should explain itself), and the commercial product is called Zest, (equally self-explanatory). Two tablets a day is the recommended dosage and I think you will find they cost you slightly less than a postage stamp.

There are several other ginseng and vitamin products, some of which are combined with the B vitamins to alleviate understandable stress. Once again it is worth remembering Oystertone is rich in zinc, so if in doubt take one of these and a Zest before a hopeful date. Take two of each if your regular partner is showing signs of irritability and you know the reason why.

If, on the other hand, your wife/lover seems to have an excessive number of disinterested headaches, the vitamins should work both ways. Should headaches continue, your worst suspicions may be confirmed.

**Brewers' enthusiasm**

Often known as Nine Pints Beautiful. This usually occurs to the young and/or free-roving agent who is feeling fit, excessively healthy and randy. He meets a lady of similar disposition and they spend the night proving the above tendencies. Having performed a series of Olympic gymnastics, a certain amount of exhaustion can set in around dawn.

It is a cruel hour, and a gentleman remembering an early

THE MIRACLE
ANTI-DROOP

appointment at the office can find himself feeling more filled with anxieties than lust.

This is not surprising; his zinc reserve has gone with the semen and the sweat of his labours, added to which his brain is dehydrated from the alcohol. The perspiration (ladies do not sweat) that has caused her make-up to look such a mess in the morning light has cost her her zinc allowance too.

Effervescent vitamin C, a compleat vitamin B, 10 mg of chelated zinc or an Oystertone, and enough geniality will be restored for at least a polite goodbye in the morning.

Having such preparations at hand could be considered either calculating or optimistic but Be Prepared was always a good motto before going out on the hunt.

For nicer occasions, like honeymoons and the beginning of a love affair, the same prescription will help combat complete sexual exhaustion.

**Alcoholic insomnia**

This is a dodgy sympton as it definitely points to real alcoholic dependence. The early riser is not neccessarily as full of virtue as would seem apparent; the inability to sleep can be the result of 'raw', undernourished nerves, a chronic restlessness that is basically due to lack of vitamin B. This person may be at work before anyone else, but the chances are that he will also be at the trough as soon as the doors open. Megadoses of vitamin B complex will soothe the nervous system during the day, and spirits should be avoided. Beer contains vitamin B and takes longer to go through the system. The alcoholic insomniac is invariably abed before anyone else, but his sleep is more likely to be of the passing-out nature. This isn't real sleep; the bloodstream is so full of it that the alcohol passes the blood-brain barrier and enters the brain. The result is a form of coma — and being comatose is hardly healthy. When such a pattern has set in, by all means use the unconventional hours; but do take vitamin C on waking to clear the toxics, and multivitamins

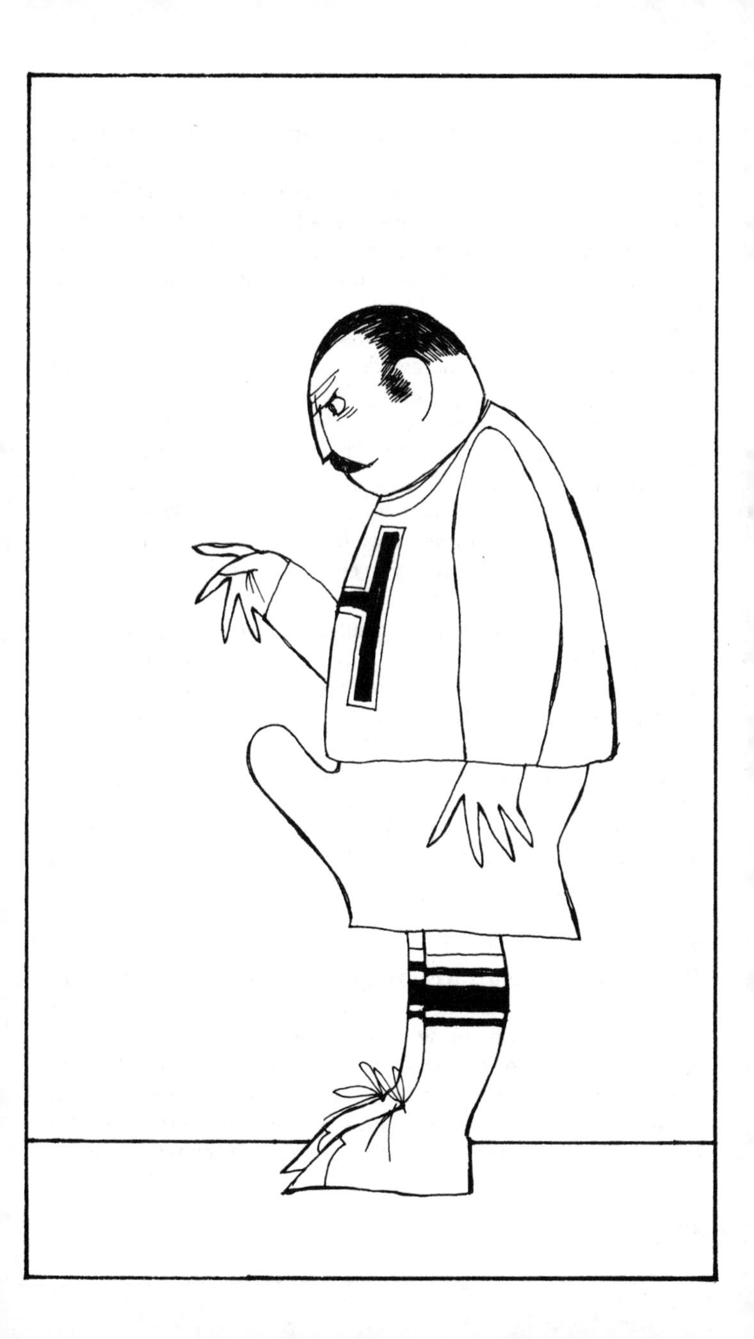

night and morning, otherwise you can suffer from malnutrition both from sleep deprivation and the lack of energy to eat properly. Try taking extra vitamin B plus Chamomile, and chelated calcium and magnesium before you get into bed to watch television. Also try using that early morning energy to get to the healthfood store — it opens a good two hours before the pub.

The other form of alcoholic insomnia occurs to those who have decided to take a few days off the booze; two fairly restless nights and they usually decide to go back on it again. That nightcap calls along with all the other temptations; not a great deal wrong with that. The body has rid itself of the marathon intake (particularly if you remembered to take the garlic perles) and feels as flash as a bookful of Green Shield stamps. The only thing is, it wasn't neccessary to spend two nights tossing and turning; you could have taken a nice little herbal sedative called Quiet Life. You will probably fall asleep reading its contents; quaint little Olde English remedies like motherwort, skullcap and valerian. Try not to dwell on what happened to those wise women when they were accused of being witches; just concentrate on the pagan festivals and partake of sweet dreams.

Alternatively you could try a sleep-inducing Hop Pillow, an historical remedy much favoured by past monarchs. They are available with all the usual variety of fillings — feathers, down or polyester — from large healthfood and departments stores.

**The Trots**

Diarrhoea frequently occurs after a desperate attempt to alleviate a ravenous hunger after the pubs have closed. A 'take-away' sign on the way home can be very beguiling — until the terrible gut-ache in the morning. Magnified by several pints of bitter the previous night, the morning experience can be less than totally charming. Nothing that a couple of tablespoonsful of kaolin and chlorodyne (and a lot of loud moaning and groaning) won't ease within the hour. Walking would help, but you daren't take the risk; so pad up and down your place of abode like a caged tiger until your stomach has stopped calling you names.

Then take an avocado, slice it in half, remove the stone and fill both cavities with a garlic-flavoured vinaigrette (olive oil, wine vinegar, crushed garlic, salt and pepper). Eat both halves of the soothing, tasty, welcome flesh and give thanks. Avocados are very nutritious, contain lots of restorative minerals as well as the important vitamins. Your nether regions will show their gratitude by ceasing to burn like a witch's cauldron. A carton of natural yoghurt (without fruit) taken later and your intestines will have their own private interflora system restored.

Persistent diarrhoea means something more fundamental is wrong. You are just not eating enough of the proper foods. You need to add a lot more high-fibre foods to your diet to prevent every bit of goodness that goes into your body being sluiced away. High fibre is the new-fangled name for good old-fashioned roughage like wholemeal bread, chicken, fish, liver, nuts, baked beans, potatoes, cabbage and raw apples. A week of eating solids plus plain yoghurt to keep the intestines healthy and you'll soon be enjoying the morning movement a lot more.

**Bruises**

These often appear from apparently nowhere on the person of the heavy drinker. They can be the result of bumping into doors or walls, falling up or down stairs, during the analgesic state. They are an indication of severe shortage of vitamin C and their disappearance will be speeded by the consumption of one gram night and morning over the top of your daily requirements. Should you remember that bruises are the result of an altercation with an acquaintance, shut the door and follow the restorative health regimen for a couple of days.

If it was your fault, promise to keep on taking the vitamins; if it was his, you will soon feel strong enough to go out and thump him.

**Bloodshot eyes**

Not a pretty sight, and though they can be treated cosmetically (blue eye-drops from any chemist work an instant miracle) this will not take care of the long-term strain of time spent in smoke-filled rooms consuming booze. Alcohol dilates small blood vessels, and that includes the ones in the eyes as well as those on the cheeks, which partly explains the boiled-in-oil appearance of the permanent tippler.

Although the blue eye-drops temporarily contract the blood vessels, it is really a shortage of vitamin A that is making itself felt. The quickest route to recovery comes, once again, from an old herbal remedy based on a plant called eyebright, appropriately enough. Eyebright can be bought in healthfood stores and comes complete with added vitamins A, B2, and D; so if you want the whites of your eyes to gleam like a detergent ad, this is the one for you. Anyone working all day under artificial light needs to take care of their eyes; temporary eye-strain after a hard day's work can be eased by the excellent Crystal Eye-drops obtainable from D.R. Harris of St James's Street, London SW1.

**Broken bones**

They say that God looks after children and drunks, but there are the odd occasions when He seems to have been looking the other way. Should such a miserable injustice happen to you, take 500-1000 mg of calcium and 400 IU of vitamin D daily, or bonemeal tablets with added vitamin D, and confound both doctors and regulars with your early return to health. You will, of course, have promised yourself that it will never happen again, and are now a convert to the vitamins regimen. Broken bones bloody hurt.

### Bad breath

White-wine drinkers please note — your best friends may not tell you, but if you see them walking away in droves it is time for you to act. I don't like to be personal, but anyone who drinks a lot of white wine gives off an odour like a headful of rotting — teeth although the smell actually comes from the stomach. Take chlorophyll tablets and chelated zinc tablets three times a day, or try a digestive like Floris by Healthcrafts, which contains *Acidophilus*, a source of friendly intestinal bacteria.

### Black eyes, cuts, scratches and grazes

All are occupational hazards for Hooligans, which can lead to embarrassing explanations. Physically you need a combination of massive doses of organic vitamin C, at least one gram, 1000 IU of vitamin E, and chelated zinc; these will help speed the healing process. I'm afraid the scratches on your back will have to remain your own psychological problem — you could try rushing out and buying a box of snuff and several white tee-shirts and pretending you have developed the most appalling cold, but I wouldn't bank on it. While in this state of disgrace you could ponder the source of aggression that got you into trouble, and decide to have a massive assault on the vitamins B. On the other hand, you could just change your friends.

### Jet-lag

Business travel is one of the toughest games Hooligans have to play, involving hard work, hard play and sleep disorientation. This really puts the vitamins to the test, so pack them first before panic and anxiety set in.

If the actual flying gives you the heeby-jeebies, try double dosing on B6 and Chamomile; this both feeds the nerves and calms you down — thus avoiding the need for half a bottle of brandy, which will only aggravate the dehydration that is part of flying anyway. We cannot all be as grand as a friend of mine who stops off at Fortnum and Mason on his way to the airport, gathering up a hamper of nourishing grub to sustain him on the journey; but a decent meal before setting off will decimate the need to eat that nutritionless crap airways proffer to relieve the boredom.

If your business meetings are likely to involve you in strenuous getting-to-know-you type drinking bouts, pack the following, and make sure you take the combination before, during and after each session.

*Concoction for survival:*
One gram vitamin C.
One megadose vitamin B complex.
Two Aminochel zinc tablets.

It doesn't matter if you have to use alcohol to get them down you, but they will keep you on your feet, keep your concentration going and the good name of your firm afloat. Take the precaution of laying out the late-night dose beside a glass of water before you leave your hotel room.

In the mornings take your multivitamins, ginseng, vitamin E or Oystertone according to your usual pattern.

On the return flight start in again on the vitamin B plus Chamomile. If your trip has been successful you will be facing envy and suspicion from colleagues, let alone the homestead, if it has been a failure you will need all your patience not to kick them in their sympathetic, smiling teeth.

**Alcoholic amnesia**

What may at first appear to be a blessing in disguise is in fact quite dangerous. What you are really suffering from at that particularly unmemorable moment is straightforward alcoholic poisoning — and that's about as sensible as taking arsenic. It happens for the simple reason that you are putting booze into the body faster than the body can deal with it.

Since it takes the system approximately eight hours to deal with the first drink of the day a solid four or five hours on the sozzle means that there is an awful lot of alcohol queuing up to be metabolised, and some of it has got into the brain. Vitamins, minerals and food speed up the metabolic processes, thus protecting the brain — which will be damaged if the situation is not corrected. A good old clean-out is what is really required, using garlic perles, vitamin C and multivitamins. Try ginseng plus vitamin E as part of your daily routine, and don't forget that chelated zinc.

Unfortunately amnesia is usually regarded as a bit of a joke, but it is actually a sign of the kind of deep malnutrition that can lead to life-long abstinence, so start taking care.

**Obesity**

The need for slimming is more likely to be the problem of a Healthy Hooligan than an unhealthy one, all down to the fact that he or she eats well too. No doubt about it, cutting out the booze works, but the very thought makes most people's drinking hand twitch. Doctors' recommendations apart, there are a couple of healthfood aids on the market that are supposed to help the good intentions along.

Spirulina is made from natural plankton, and is said to contain all the vitamins, minerals and proteins the human needs for survival. Sinisterly enough, both Spirulina and Oystertone have been developed mainly through the search for a survival food in case of the nuclear holocaust; a cynical and saddening thought that those who are contemplating destroying the earth are at last discovering the wondrous, elemental gifts of our environment.

Yes, well, enough of that; what interests you is how the stuff helps you slim. Apart from containing more amino acids than you or I have heard of, Spirulina also obliges with one called phenylalanine. This acts directly on the appetite centre of the brain in such a way that you can take in half the

Squeezing an Orange – the Charles Atlas Method.

amount of tuck without feeling deprived. I have not checked whether its miracle qualities can make a small drink look as satisfying as a large.

The other magic slimmer is kelp, which comes from seaweed, and also happens to contain more minerals and vitamins, weight for weight, than any other food. It has long been used in controlling obesity, and is usually combined with cider vinegar. It can be bought in tablet form at healthfood stores.

# The Sexual Athlete.

# SURVIVAL FOR SINNERS

# SURVIVAL FOR SINNERS

Invaluable in performing rescue operations, vitamins can also help and sustain us in working to the best of our ability and combatting the stresses of the job in hand. I wouldn't like to claim that they would get you the Chairman's job within the week, but they can ease the strain of the climb and leave you with energy for the more important things in life — being yourself, having a laugh, getting laid or whatever.

Here is a brief list of the sorts of job that can deplete the system — and how to prevent them from doing so. Any vitamins mentioned should be taken on top of the usual drinking, smoking and general neglect allowance.

**Performing artistes**
Definitely you need all the vitamins B every single day, preferably in high-potency, slow-release form. Take B6 plus Chamomile to calm the nerves for auditions and first nights. If embarking on a long run, try out ginseng during rehearsals. Actresses on the Pill should look out for a brand of products called Ladycare, designed to put back what the Pill takes out, but they are advised to take extra B6 if they are inclined to screaming matches the week before their period is

due. Efomal is another brand that contains oil of evening primrose and is good for the skin, menstrual regularity and keeps the cholesterol count from going up — always a danger when on tour.

Musicians who stay up all night should look to their vitamins A and D to counteract staying in bed all day; if member of pop group and surrounded by ardent female fans, it would be wise to take ginseng plus vitamins E and B6 — you never know when one of those girls is going to sell her story to the newspapers.

Singers need to protect the precious larynx with masses of vitamin C, preferably using the organic kind for extra immunity from infection.

Dancers would do well to remember to replace the zinc they sweat out during each performance, otherwise they might be too exhausted to have a drink afterwards.

**Travelling salesman**

Driving is an exhausting business which calls for high-potency slow-release vitamins B. If your food intake comes mainly from Greasy-Spoon type cafés you would do well to look out for a product called Lecithin, which will mop up the fat that would otherwise either float round your bloodstream or settle in your liver. Should those tales of bored housewives greeting the travelling salesman in nothing more than a negligée be true, add 400 IU of vitamin E to your daily intake. Any salesman over thirty or on an established, demanding beat should increase this dosage — anything up to 1000 IU will be okay; add plenty of vitamin C to counteract minor infections. The major ones are your own problem. If your job involves whoopee-style conferences, keep a supply of the combination recommended in the Jet-lag section — you never know when that total recall (when all about you were falling over) might come in useful.

**Writers, seamstresses and gamblers**
All good candidates for Eyebright with vitamins A and D, these — seamstresses for the fine and accurate stitching which strains the eyes; writers to counteract the aching glare of a piece of blank white paper waiting to be decorated with words of wit and wisdom; gamblers to neutralize the effect of staring at roulette wheels and packs of cards, earnestly willing the right numbers to come up.

Gamblers on a losing streak should add vitamins B plus Chamomile to relieve their anxiety and get a good night's sleep. Writers, who will doubtless have sought those words hiding in the bottom of a bottle, will need megadoses of vitamin C and Mega-B-Complex, with extra B12 to resist snapping at wives, lovers, editors and publishers or kicking the dog.

Since all three occupations require long hours indoors, these Hooligans should add 1000 IU of vitamin E to discourage degeneration of muscles useful for walking to pub, club or bank.

**Top executives and bank managers**
Wanted — additional high-life vitamins to deal with those expense-account lunches; all those exquisite dishes swimming in butter followed by several large brandies can increase the cholesterol level. Lecithin and kelp will help keep the weight down and cleanse the blood and liver of fatty substances.

Executives could benefit from a course of ginseng with vitamin E and vitamin B6 for mental alertness coupled with calm. Overdraft owners would be very grateful if their bank managers take Stress-B-Complex when promises of repayment go unfulfilled; it could help prevent panic and threats of cutting us off without a shilling.

Both groups should take the Boozers' Regimen (one gram vitamin C, one tablet vitamins B compleat plus two

Aminochel zinc) before embarking on any lunch that is designed to seduce money out of them.

**Teachers**
Definitely high-potency, slow-release vitamins B with breakfast to feed the nervous system before facing a roomful of recalcitrant kids and, even more definitely, another one in the evening before departing for the pub for a replay of kindergarten behaviour.

**Strippers**
Probably not many problems about slimming — all that rushing from club to club and gyrating therein; but Spirulina, which provides proteins and minerals, will help keep you fit if a hasty sandwich is all you can grab. I would recommend vitamin E, 1000 IU, for your own sense of sexuality if it becomes demoralised by the listless, indifferent customers. If you have to drink crappy champagne with said customers, insist on adding Guinness to it; Black Velvet is chic and full of vitamins

**Policemen**
There is something you can do about looking younger to half the population; get rid of the spots that come from over-cooked canteen food. Apprehend at least one gram of vitamin C a day. Take high-potency slow-release vitamin B if you are on the beat in a dodgy area; it will soothe the nerves and keep that level of tolerance the Police Force needs for its good name. It may even give you the patience to fill in all those damn' forms.

**Builders, miners, labourers**
Fighting persistent pollution, dust and dirt are your chief problems. You need extra vitamin A for your lungs and eyes. Vitamins C and E will help revitalise the body if you are working in any sort of fumes all day. Add vitamin B for the

strain on your nerves if working in a noisy occupation like scaffold-building or pneumatic drilling; you may think you enjoy the antisocial row you kick up, but you are still exhausting your resources.

**Eternal Peter Pans**

With the emphasis on youth these days, most strivers want to clip a few years from their latest score. If your career (or your sex appeal) has always been dependent on your bright good looks, you will need all the following vitamins to maintain your charm through to late middle age.

Obviously vitamin E, 1000 IU daily, plus RNA/DNA nucleic acid tablets, (100 mg) for cell regeneration and keeping the youthful bloom on the skin.

Since EPPs always want to be in the swim, you will also need a good three grams of vitamin C a day plus all the vitamins B for energy. Eyes being the first part of the body to show tiredness and an indication of age, take Eyebright three times daily. And, as there is no sight more ridiculous and pathetic than an ageing Hooligan exhausted-pissed (or fast asleep, whichever way you want to put it) in a nightclub, do remember the Boozers' Regimen, before, during and after drinking. The during and after part of the Regimen may be crucial if those boyish/girlish good looks have done the trick.

**Wives, husbands, lovers of Hooligans**

Well, you said for Better or for Worse, but living with one of these charming bastards can be a strain even though life will never be dull. Look after yourself first — it is the only way you will survive the course.

Take megadoses of vitamins C, B-complex plus B6 for stress and vitamin E so the worry won't affect your looks. Take a multivitamin daily for your minerals. All these will help prevent you rising to the bait when the Dread Hooligan comes home looking for a row, and give you the energy you'll need when the same Hooligan wants to go out and celebrate.

Keep a storecupboard full of vitamins for all contrite and reasonable moments, and smuggle as much natural food into the Hooligan as you possibly can. Mineral water in the fridge is bound to get used and bran in casseroles will be swallowed unnoticed.

Buy this book and let them realise they are living with a saint.

**Smokers**

Apart from ensuring you take enough vitamin C to cover the daily cigarette consumption (each cigarette depletes the body of 25 mg of vitamin C, the amount contained in one orange, so a packet of twenty uses up 500 mg a day). Thus you need at least a gram a day, more if intending see a few men about a dog.

Obviously it isn't my job to tell people what kind of cigarette they should smoke, but those new throw-away filters do reveal that some very nasty gunge gets into the lungs, so they are worth a thought. A packet of ten lasts about three packets of fags and costs about the price of one.

There is also a brand-new product on the market that is designed to protect the tissues of the lungs, especially from the great dread — lung cancer. It is called Beta-Carotene, related to the vitamin A and is designed to protect the lungs from attack by carcinogens. It is made by Healthcrafts and a month's supply costs slightly more than three packets of cigarettes. If the tax on cigarettes goes any higher the pills will appear to cost even less, if you see what I mean.

**Politicians**

It would doubtless be of invaluable service to the country as a whole if one of the ten rumoured bars in the Houses of Parliament were converted into a healthfood store; then they could all take ginseng to keep them from falling asleep during important debates. They should all be taking megadoses of vitamins B, not so much for the work they do as the strain of

giving and receiving abuse continuously. Certainly masses of vitamin C to combat those hours spent wandering the corridors of power looking for the other bars. And if only half the scandalous gossip is correct, quite a few of them should be on Vitamin E to support the clandestine spending of energies.

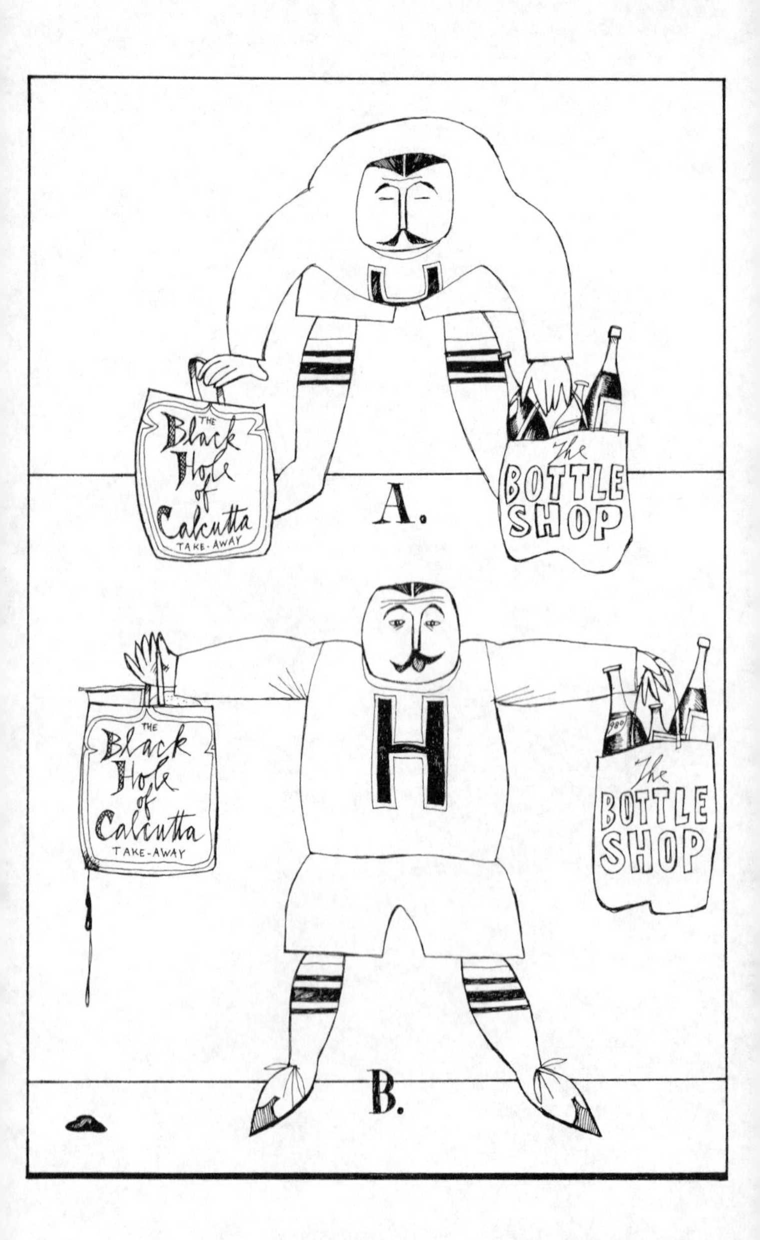
THE Black Hole of Calcutta
TAKE-AWAY
The BOTTLE SHOP
A.
THE Black Hole of Calcutta
TAKE-AWAY
The BOTTLE SHOP
B.

# HARVEST FESTIVAL

# HARVEST FESTIVAL

Apart from drink and vitamins, there is another small thing we need for survival. It is called Food.

Now your average drinking person, who is usually generous to a fault when it comes to financing a large round, is often quite reluctant to part with the sovereigns on something so mundane as groceries. It is a grievous fault, I admit, but one that can be corrected with a certain degree of compromise. After all, there is nothing so depressing as coming home late at night with a skinful, feeling absolutely ravenous, to find nothing more than a stale or moulding crust in the larder and a somewhat tatty-looking tomato in the fridge.

This particular scenario usually depicts a life that has recently undergone a rather serious period of self-neglect, not to mention a rather splendid period of self-indulgence. We are definitely due for a few days of Remorse and Resolution.

Start by turning out the pockets or handbag where you will doubtless find a profusion of change from the notes that sped across the bar with such a flourish. The Hooligan mind will probably calculate swiftly how many drinks such a sum will buy, even though the Hooligan body will be protesting that

EALTH
FOOD

what it needs most in the world right now is Grub.

This is where the compromise comes in. Like all strokes of genius, it is quite simple. You only buy food that is actually going to do you good. You do not spend precious drinking money on junk like tinned vegetables, instant anything and blotting-paper masquerading as bread. If you are going to be forced to part with money, you might as well get value for it.

The walk to the shops will probably be pure Hell — but then so would the walk to the pub. It will be slightly less hellish if you have some idea of your needs, so I have produced some guidelines. Come to think of it, you might as well take your cheque book and card along with you and do the lot in one fell swoop. You can always take a cab back, make it wait while you unload, then take it on to the pub for a heart-starter; at least you will have supplies at home.

Obviously the kind of area you live in will dictate how many shops you have to visit; if you are lucky and have one of the better supermarkets on hand, life will be a lot simpler. If your odyssey involves going to the butcher, the baker and the rest, go first to the chemist and get hold of some vitamins B. At this stage you have no need to be fussy; swallow brewers' yeast (and try not to let the name make you nostalgic) by the handful if that is all they have, or take twice the dosage of any brand of B complex. These will help support you when the woman in front of you in the queue cannot make up her mind whether she wants half a pound of lambs' tongues or a bull's ball. Try and hang on for your pound of mince and your sausages, because they are going to be your lifesavers. N.B. The noise of the till ringing will be excruciating, but this is your Day of Resolution, remember?

So now let's concentrate on the essentials for your storecupboard.

**Bread**
The Staff of Life it used to be called, though nowadays some of it is about as supportive as a used straw. *Wholemeal bread* is what you need to buy. Wholemeal bread contains vitamins B1 and B6; it is good for the nerves, helps settle the shakes and generally aids concentration. It also provides natural vitamin E, which fights both fatigue and your cholestorol count, and contains life-sustaining minerals too. All brown bread is not necessarily wholemeal, so look at the label if you are buying in a supermarket and ask for it specifically at the baker's. *Granary bread* is delicious but it is not always made with wholemeal flour, the best of which proudly announces that it is stoneground. You might as well get the best while you are at it. Never bother with sliced white unless you want to be a nutrition delinquent.

**Bran**
This may sound like a new-fangled fad because of all the high-fibre hype, but it really is a bloody good way of looking after your body cheaply. A couple of tablespoonsful a day could keep the out-patients room at bay. Allinson Natural Bran Plus can be bought at Boots and can be shoved into anything — stews, stuffing for poultry, hamburgers, sprinkled over breakfast cereals, into soups (even tinned ones), popped into spaghetti sauces or added to coatings for frying fish.

Bran also contains the vitamins B and E and, by keeping the colon healthy, maintains the body at maximum health. It is also claimed to be a positive factor in preventing heart disease and cancer of the colon. For the Hooligan it is one of the least painful paths to health invented. A month's supply costs a few pence more than a virgin tonic. Do buy it.

**Lentils**
Very, very useful parcels of pure benefit. It doesn't matter which sort you buy, they are all full of proteins (those things

that will make you grow up to be a big boy like yer mum), minerals and vitamins. All you have to do for a restorative and easy-to-swallow meal is soak them for half an hour or half a day according to your own recovery programme, then bung them in a saucepan with quite a lot of water, a couple of cloves of garlic, an onion and whatever herbs you have about the place. Leave them to simmer for an hour or so and you will have a comforting meal that gives the body a glow of nourishment; if you add the bran you can have real virtue thrown in. Make enough to put in the fridge to come back home to sometime. You can add a packet of frozen vegetables to liven it up.

They do say that leaving a dish of raw lentils in cold water for a few days will produce a highly edifying crop of sprouts (a bit like a mustard and cress experiment) which, munched fresh, will provide you with vitamins B, E, C and A. Why not? *Bean sprouts* as in Chinese food are rich in vitamin C. Healthfood stores also sell a selection of sprouting seeds including the traditional miracle nature healers — *alfalfa, sunflower seed* and *fenugrek*. At least if you don't get home for three days there will be something fresh and healthy waiting for you when you do.

## Honey

Another good standby, easy to take even if it's only in your morning cup of tea. It seems to have a million healing, soothing qualities. If your throat is raw from too many cigarettes, or talking too loudly and long the night before, a dessertspoonful taken neat or in a little warm water will work comforting wonders. If you have been overworking, a spoonful in a cup of warm milk at night gives you both calcium and a good night's sleep. Paradoxically, it is also a source of instant energy and a lot better for you than a choc bar.

**Nuts**
I know it sounds like another daft idea, but they are full of protein, vitamins A and B and minerals, so once again the hunger-struck Hooligan might as well have them at hand or at least devour them if out taking a cocktail. Mind you, if they are salted they will only make you thirstier and we all know where that leads. Still, they are slightly more nourishing than those glazed eyes on toast.

**Yoghurt**
Frightfully good for the nether end. Well, what goes in must come out, and while it is going through its natural process it might as well do you a bit of good. It prevents harmful bacteria taking up lodgings (I was going to say squatters' rights but it does sound a little uncouth), and is also allegedly responsible for extreme longevity in Georgia, Russia, and remote parts of Bulgaria. Not a pleasing thought for an outrageous Westerner (we'd probably spend 120 years in jail) but, added to a *chilli con carne* or the breakfast scramble in the liquidiser, yoghurt can set up your unmentionables a treat.

**Cooking oil**
If the only thing that can get the body on the feet of a morning is the prospect of a solid fried breakfast, do make sure you use a vegetable oil like Mazola which is a *corn oil*, or any of the other high-polyunsaturate oils like *safflower, peanut* or *sesame*. Time to look out for that cholesterol count again. It's the animal fats in you that cause the harm, so watch it.

**Beans**
Yes, they do mean . . . but even the most puritanical healthfood freak cannot deny the value of tinned baked beans. They contain protein and roughage (high fibre to the posh) so stock up on them. Eat them on a slice of wholemeal bread and you will have done yourself the favour of the day.

Add them to a homemade minestrone made with chopped onions, green peppers and carrots and you may almost be excused supper so long as you take your other vitamins. Beans in any form are Red Cross food. Look out for *soy bean* products to keep in the store cupboard. They look a bit like dogfood, but the soy bean has more than twice the protein value of a steak weight for weight, and if you add it to your cottage pie you will be gaining the good old energy-giving natural food your body has been begging for. *Red kidney beans* are another good source of ballast for the days when you don't actually feel like facing the world. They are the basis of *chilli con carne*, another meal that doubles up on good lasting value for very little money.

*Kidney beans* have the same virtues as the rest of their family; vitamins, minerals, protein and roughage. But they do have one very painful disadvantage. They are very hard, and consequently extremely noisy as they make their passage from package to basin in which to be soaked. I have solved that problem for those so dangerously delicate in the morning that a net curtain stirring can afford the traumatic effect of a street mugging; you put the water in the basin first. Beans then obligingly slither and silently swell until they are ready to be transferred to saucepan and boiled without mercy for fifteen minutes. Make sure the saucepan is large enough for you to leave the kitchen for this period. If you do not boil them for this time there is something about their enzymes which will ensure it is *your* body that will produce the loud noises you were so anxious to avoid. You will need a fleet of juggernauts changing gear to cover your embarrassment as you walk up the street.

That precaution taken care of, all you need to do to make sure you are properly nourished for the week is to fry onions, green pepper and that pound of mincemeat, all together in vegetable oil with two teaspoonsful of chili powder, and add a small tin of tomato purée. Add a pint or so of water, the usual garlic and herbs, and bung it in the oven till you feel strong enough to take it out. I am, of course, taking it for granted that you have cooked before, so leave the oven on low if you contemplate going out for just the one. Should some long-hoped-for friend or enemy appear, your late meal will do you just as much good even if it is eaten at four in the morning.

**Seeds**

Lastly, try keeping small packets of *sunflower, pumpkin* and *sesame seeds* on the shelf. I know it may sound like I've gone stark, staring mad, but they are superbly good for you and very tasty too. A little bowlful mixed together to nibble while you watch any old crap on the television on an Absolutely Dread Day and you will be feeding yourself a perfect form of protein, vitamins A, C, E and the Bs plus a selection of essential minerals. And they are not even half as noisy as a packet of crisps.

**Other things worth stocking**

*Crispbreads* for the days you run out of bread.
*Peanut butter* for vitamins B and minerals.
*Dried milk,* no reason, just useful.
*Tuna fish* contains selenium, a mineral that males lose when they have been at it all night. If you see a macho fella boasting and eating a tuna-fish sandwich, he is probably telling the truth.
*Sardines, salmon,* good for the teeth, bones and pulse.
*Eggs,* rich in iron, vitamins A, E, B1, B2 and B12 — no wonder we all reach for them on the morning after.
*Cheese* has calcium for strong teeth and bones, also vitamins B2 and B12.
*Butter* for vitamin D.
*Margarine* for vitamins A and D.
*Raisins* for vitamins B and natural sugar.
*Marmite* for vitamins B, to spread on wholemeal toast or add to soups.

Naturally you will add your own fads and fancies to this list, but try not to waste too much money on empty foods, though a few packets of instant soup to which you can add your bran could be a useful provision for a nourishing nightcap on the not-all-bad evenings.

Arm yourself with a packet of cling-film and silver foil for storage, and you have equipped yourself with some basic life-sustainers to continue working and playing hard.

**Vegetables and fruits**

Now you need some fresh foods from the greengrocer or market.

*Potatoes,* delicous, comforting spuds, for boiling or baking (frying destroys their vitamins). Since their vitamin C is stored just below the skin it is absolutely lethal to peel them. Buy yourself one of those green plastic scouring pads and use it to clean them; it is almost effortless. Buy spuds weekly and keep them wrapped in newspaper or a brown paper bag; exposure to light ruins their vitamin content.

*Onions,* rich in selenium again, so take to the onion soup when the love-life becomes exhausting. Could this be why the French are so fond of it? Pickled onions will not have the same effect either before or after; this is nothing to do with the smell on the breath, just that the processing depletes the precious selenium.

*Garlic;* in my opinion anyone who objects to the smell of garlic emanating from another is not a fit companion for a Hooligan. Nevertheless, apart from the consumption of snails in garlic butter, it isn't neccessary for garlic to regurgitate and knock your neighbour back a couple of feet. Crushed and added to stews that contain carrots and parsley, garlic can give you all the benefit of its flavour plus the knowledge that you are taking in vitamins C and B and cleansing your blood with what is known in the Soviet Union as 'Russian Penicillin'.

*Cabbage,* well known as the drinkers friend, it contains potassium which is what you are short of on those days when

you are feeling utterly lethargic and weak. It gathers up the garbage and directs oxygen to the brain in a most efficient manner. Shredded and cooked in a little water for three to four minutes with a little butter, salt and pepper added, and even those who feel death is preferable to food will rally. Or add a chicken bouillon cube and more liquid and turn it into soup; the effect will be the same and you will taking in some vitamin C and the nerve-balming B6.
*Green peppers*, choc-a-block with vitamin C.
*Tomatoes*, ditto.
*Broccoli*, another great source of selenium.
*Leafy greens* of all kinds, rich in vitamin E, calcium and potassium.
*Citrus fruits*, all excellent sources of vitamin C and potassium.
*Cantaloupe melon*, very high in vitamin A as well as C and B6. Another good one for the potassium content, and loaded with other essential minerals.
*Peaches, apricots*, plenty of iron.
*Bananas*, also very high in potassium — probably why they make such a good breakfastfood. Put two tablespoonsful bran, one banana, carton of plain yoghurt and a dessertspoonful of honey into the liquidiser and use the drink to wash down your vitamin supplements. If you have a long journey ahead and are unlikely to get a decent lunch, add a couple of tablespoonsful of powdered protein; you can buy it from major chemist chains as well as at healthfood stores.

It is a fact that fish, liver and kidneys are important — but it is also a fact that they are difficult to shop for and get home in a state fit to eat, so try to fit them in to any meals out. They are rich in all the vitamins B, particularly B12. Beef and pork are also good sources of vitamin B12; but in any case a variety of meats is needed as a source of protein supplies.

Intelligent vegetarians will not be needing my advice on how to supplement their diet.

**Water**

W.C. Fields may have had unkind things to say about water ('Fish fuck in it') but it is a fact that we need it to live. More than half our body weight is made up of water, and it is essential to keep our insides on the move. Six to eight glasses a day are needed — though what we put in it is our own business. Because of its dehydrating effect, deciding on alcohol means that we need more liquid so (apart from putting extra water in your drinks) it's not a bad idea to take a glass of the pure stuff from time to time, just to give the kidneys a helping hand. Well, you wouldn't let your loo get blocked, now, would you?

Mineral Waters are not a con. They are very, very good for you, and are meticulously supervised by the governments of the countries they come from. They are as distant from tapwater as a reprobate is from a saint. They have varying qualities and tastes, but their main function is to flush out the system and cleanse the kidneys. Many of them are never exported from their native lands, but below is a list of some of those more familiar on these shores.

*From France*

Evian Water comes from the Haut Savoie mountains in the French Alps and is the product of mountain rain and melted snow. It is a still water of great purity, excellent on its own when the body doth protest from too much of everything, and is great for the kidneys. It is also the perfect complement to fine whiskies, lightening the richness without interfering with the flavour.

Perrier Water is a highly effervescent, naturally carbonated water that can truly do wonders for the dehydrated body and brain. It is like taking a shower on the inside and just as stimulating, good for the digestion in general and especially for anyone with a tendency towards up-chucking. Brandy drinkers who take theirs neat would do well to sluice out the stomach with Perrier to avoid the inflammation that can lead

to alcoholic gastritis. It also has the advantage of being a socially acceptable drink amongst even the most severe social drinkers and, as it moves through the system fast, it very quickly eliminates yesterday's waste.
Vichy Water — a slightly sparkling water with a bit of a salty taste, very good for the liver, particularly after a day on the red wine when one is inclined to feel a bit weighed down; this is due to the resins in the wine, which have a tendency to hang around. Vichy is an antacid too, so good for heartburn.
Vittel Water — a still water that stimulates the kidneys to get rid of waste products, it is also excellent for sufferers from gout, rheumatism and arthritis.

*From Italy*
San Pellegrino is a lightly bubbling water that has added carbon dioxide. Also very refreshing and good for the kidneys, especially recommended for anyone suffering from cystitus, a misery-making infection of the bladder, alas often the result of too much alchohol and not enough vitamins. Said to be good for gout and eczema too.

*From Germany*
Apollinaris Water — rather a strong salty, sparkling water, full of natural minerals, all very therapeutic.

*From Great Britain*
Sainsbury's bottle their own mineral water from a spring in Shropshire. Needless to say, its purity is guaranteed.
Ashe Park Water, straight from a natural spring in Hampshire and available at healthfood stores.
Highland Spring Water comes from a spring in the foothills of the Ochils in Perthshire; available in both still and sparkling form.

**Eating out**

This can be a pleasure or a pain, as much depending on the circumstances as the quality of the restaurant. Business lunches can be killers if the digestive juices are all screwed up by anxiety; those of a highly sensitive disposition (that's us, dear) will frequently have pre-empted the ordeal by tanking up the night before, especially if our future hangs on such an invitation. The effort of trying to hide the abject state plus awareness of loss of concentration (you have forgotten everything you planned to say and rehearsed saying last night) can result in an unaccustomed clumsiness and hypocritical desire to please.

You should, of course, have taken a vitamin B plus Chamomile, but the mere search for a clean shirt or pair of tights and the fear of being late threw you. Then along comes the waiter with a menu you know is going to waver in your hand like the Royal Standard atop Buckingham Palace and give the whole game away.

This is where you need to know what is going to do you most good without even glancing at said stumbling block and without having to fumble for your glasses either. A swift glance round the other tables should be a sufficient guideline. Oysters for their restorative zinc and minerals should be first choice, cantaloupe for its B6 and potassium the second; or settle for half a grapefruit for its C and potassium.

Aim for a plain grilled sole, liver or lamb chops with lots of vegetables for the main course; that way you will have helped restore your zinc and offered the body lots of the other minerals that went missing the night before.

The choice of booze will doubtless depend on your host, but a request for a bottle of mineral water will not only ease your raging thrist but also prevent you from knocking back the wine as if it were water, thus becoming over-confident again too quickly.

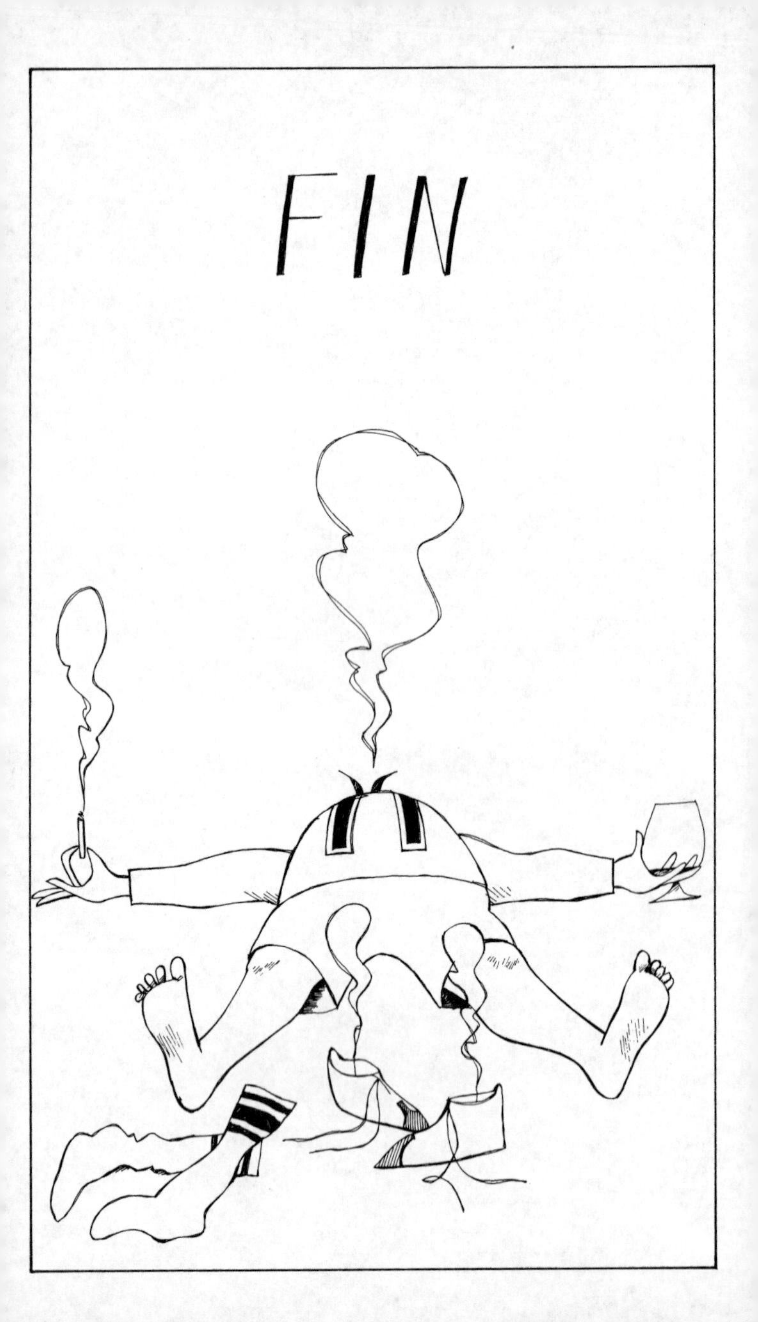
FIN

# PARADISE IN PERIL

# PARADISE IN PERIL

Enjoying a good drink is one thing; going over the top is another, and I doubt if there are many of us regular drinkers who don't suffer from the occasional twinge of anxiety whether we, too, might be heading for the gutter.

Unfortunately, that weaving wino, lurching about bottle of cheap sherry in hand or stretched oblivious across the pavement, is not much help as far as warning signals are concerned. We know we will never become like that; we have too much pride, dignity, etcetera. Or have we?

Alcohol is one of the most deceptive drugs because it is socially acceptable; even smoking has been relegated to second division, and nobody would ever admit to company at large, let alone a boss, to being hooked on heroin. So the pitfalls of booze are left to our own rather under-informed judgement.

The word 'alcoholic' has become synonymous with the incapacitated failure who cannot hold a job because he/she cannot hold the drink. In consequence, the subject becomes somewhat taboo in the comfort of the local, and any slight irregularities of behaviour can quickly draw solace and good-humoured forgiveness. Disaster is transformed into a joke, a story to be repeated, enhanced, hero-fied.

So what are the danger signals? Socially they can be divided into two categories.

In the first are those where you have made an absolute arsehole of yourself, like falling asleep in your soup at a flash dinner, picking on someone bigger than yourself and having to follow it through with a stupid scuffle outside, or the public blub of self-pity. These can usually be laughed off with a brief apology over the first drink of the following day.

The other catergory is much more serious; it is when the booze starts affecting your work. This is not a moral judgement, merely facing the need for getting the money to maintain the life-style to which you have accustomed yourself. Ringing up from the pub and pretending you are stuck in some distant town, getting a friend to ring to say an uncle has died, telling any old lie to get out of a meeting because you have over-fortified yourself for the event — all these are dangerous.

Getting your secretary to cover for you is especially dangerous, as the information may well filter through the office structure if it happens too frequently. Eventually you will run out of relatives to pop off, disaster journeys and excuses in general; your employers, clients, whatever, may well run out of patience too.

This is definitely a checkpoint moment. It may be that you despise your job or that you can justify the daily sessions by a need to keep up your contacts; but the chances are you are topping up; your system is never quite free of alcohol, more so if you are neglecting to eat properly.

The fact is that it takes the body about an hour to eliminate half a measure of spirits, half a glass of wine or a quarter of a pint of beer, so three large gins to pull you round before lunch won't be out of your system by opening time. Some people can manage it — Mother Nature has been generous with enzymes in some livers — but some people can't. Sometimes people who were very stalwart elbow-raisers for years suddenly find they can't handle it like they could in the old days. It is time to take stock, check to see how much more work you were doing five, two, years ago, and see if your lack of drive could be something to do with just a bit too much prolonged drinking. If your sex drive has gone too, the chances are you need to cut back, lay off, apply whichever discipline suits your character and circumstances. Just build up your body strength with vitamins and food, and keep an eye on your own progress.

The experts do point out that financial trouble through booze is one of the symptons of decline, and I dare say they are right; the only thing is that with the country in the state it is and most of the population either in debt or a bit short of loot, financial shame has disappeared. So if someone comes into the pub and offers you a large one, you are going to accept whether your liver likes it or not. Which brings us to another great British pitfall — the expanding round of drinks.

You can be standing in a pub nursing a modest amount, whether from virtue or necessity, when in come a couple of mates who want to throw money around. It would, of course, be churlish to refuse, so the path of good intentions has to wait until tomorrow.

I am afraid we set these traps for ourselves with all the diligence of a posse of poachers. There are no excuses. The danger lies in the speed of consumption and the allure of the company. But if your job is at stake you are going to have to pass up the occasional binge, because there is one sad, real truth and that is that pub friends soon tire of failures.

Most people who drink regularly do sometimes secretly worry about just what they are doing to themselves physically. I asked The Experts about danger signals. Not all their answers were exactly welcome, but here they are.

*Not being able to face breakfast.* Well, loss of appetite in general is a bad sign, but if your life pattern involves hours that differ from the norm you may well have eaten so late at night that you are genuinely not hungry. Breakfast may take place at lunchtime; so long as you eat something before you work or drink you should be safe. I still think that bunging fruit, yoghurt, honey and bran in the liquidiser and using the drink to wash the vitamins down is the least troublesome form of body maintenance. You can add a whole egg if the next meal is a long way off. If you regularly feel too lethargic to make even a piece of toast, The Experts could be right.

*Night sweating* means the booze has been trying to get out as desperately as you have been trying to put it in. You're probably over-loading. If you can't blame the weather, the weight of the blankets or the menopause, you'll have to accept it's the booze and do something about it. Note, too, that the disturbed nights will make you irritable, so watch over those vitamins B.

*Burns.* If as in cigarette, on fingers or funiture, very bad — you could kill yourself before the alcohol does. You might even kill others and be forcibly removed from the source of supply. You'll have to change one habit or the other. If the burns are the result of a cack-handed attempt to cook something late at night, you can take a plus-point for trying; but you can take two if you re-plan your life and make easily reheatable meals not less than once a week. This way you will at least be acknowledging the existance of food.

*Pins and needles* in hands and feet; everybody's panic button, this — usually coupled with conviction that a heart attack is imminent. Go and see your doctor, who will tell you to lay off the booze for a while; sometimes an authoritative order is easier to obey than your own common-sense. You've been over-doing it and need rest and recuperation.

*Flushed face.* This is a result of the alcohol dilating the tiny blood vessels under the skin, something that also happens when you have taken a brisk walk over the cliff tops. No, you can't get away with it; the healthy flush is a bright pink, the alcoholic flush is a decided purple. Knock off the spirits and red wine for a start, and lower the consumption before the veins burst and your pretty face is ruined forever.

*Impotence.* Do not blame on increasing age but increased intake. Do not be panicked into drinking to forget the problem. Often it can be dealt with by taking ginseng; and vitamin E combinations will help restore a gentleman's abilities even if there is no morning erection. *You* will feel better, more mentally vigorous, consequently the sun will shine brighter and the sap will rise again. It doesn't take long, but when you return to the booze, seeking a partner to share the miracle, do take it easy. Most women prefer their men to be under the sheets rather than under the table.

*Gastritis, diarrhoea, excessive heartburn;* are all signs that you are destroying the linings of your stomach and intestines. Neat spirits literally burn the insides. You can re-inflate the stomach with effervescent mineral waters or lager, but any signs of a dodgy tum must be dealt with by a doctor. Do not worry about lying to him when he asks you how much you drink; he will double your answer anyway, and can tell the truth by all the other signs. Do remember your insides are precious, ulcers miserable and operations foul. Worse still, an operation means you will be disqualified from the game for a while.

*Susceptibility to colds, 'flu, general infections.* Your body isn't getting an even break. Whisky, lemon juice and aspirin are a comforting way to withstand the initial misery, but it is only the rest that is doing you any real good. Start with massive daily doses of vitamin C and resolve to put your body in order; it is a grateful thing, and will reward you by not breaking out in boils, pustules, and rotting teeth — hardly elegant symbols of a high-flying Hooligan.

*Alcoholic amnesia.* We have all woken up at times wondering how we got home; we have even occasionally woken up to wonder who is the owner of the head on the other pillow. Sometimes discreet enquiries can solve the first puzzle. The latter situation is best tackled by exploring whether the premises (and pillow) belong to the other party or you. After that you are on your own; this is not a book of etiquette.

So we recognise that amnesia is socially dangerous, particularly if we find ourselves walking strange streets in the early dawn. Physically it ain't too healthy either, especially if there is a tendency to drink oneself deliberately into oblivion; there is the risk of becoming a drunk which is not at all the same thing as enjoying a good drink. Drinking with boring people can be a short-cut to amnesia, so check both the company you are keeping and your vitmins. A continuous high level of obliterating drink does actually kill brain cells, which can lead to an insidious loss of identity; if you forget the person you were, and all your talents and bright ideals, others forget that person too. You become what you are, and that could be rather horrible — a has-been, a bit of a wanker. Don't let it happen. If the occasional blotto session is becoming too much of a habit, do a rescue job on yourself before some institution has to.

*Personality change.* This is as much psychological as physiological. It's fine when the drink makes you bold, witty and wondrous; but when Mr or Mrs Hyde start turning up as an inherent part of your persona that you are on dangerous ground. Violence and aggression are not pretty companions (though airing a long-nurtured opinion of an acquaintance can be very satisfying); picking fights, smashing windows, imagining slights or inventing jealousies and resentments, are a sign that the booze is winning over your natural good sense. It is beating your nervous system to death and you have no resilience. Megadoses of vitamin B can help restore your sanity, sense of humour and self-regard. Try it before you lose your family and friends, and before even your foes can't be bothered to talk to you.

*Special problems for Lady Hooligans.* The Experts state that women, physically, cannot drink the same quantity as men. Well, I suppose a nine-stone woman could not consume the same amount as a sixteen-stone fella — but then neither could a seven-stone weakling. Some women can drink as well as many a man most of the time, but they have to contend with a biological factor that men don't — the menstrual cycle (and very often the Pill too). It has been recognised only recently that the Pill depletes the body of vitamin B6, and that the depletion can add to premenstrual tension or stress, (PMT). It would seem obvious for women whose job, husband's job or personal pleasure involves the partaking of alcohol should ensure a full vitamin B intake throughout the month. Statistics show that there has been an increase in the number of women amongst us suffering from alcohol-induced liver disease; the symptoms are being tired, losing weight and being unable to cope — the sort of symptoms that usually lead to a brisk prescription of tranquilisers or pull-yourself-togethers. A vulnerable liver needs vitamins not Valium.

It is a well-known fact that drink can galvanise a woman's sex drive (not for nothing do the Australians call a bottle of gin a leg-opener) but women should be warned there is a form of female impotence that can result from over-imbibing for too long; it is the dehydrated vagina. So if you are having to reach for the vaseline too often, leave the bottle alone for a while and build up on your vitamin E.

All the above are what The Experts call *risk factors*, which means that if you regularly ignore the signs you might slip into the state of chronic drinking and ruin your health, personality and career. You have been warned. It is always sensible for the regular drinker to have an annual check-up; a blood test revealing a high cholesterol count or slight malfunction of the liver can be so easily corrected.

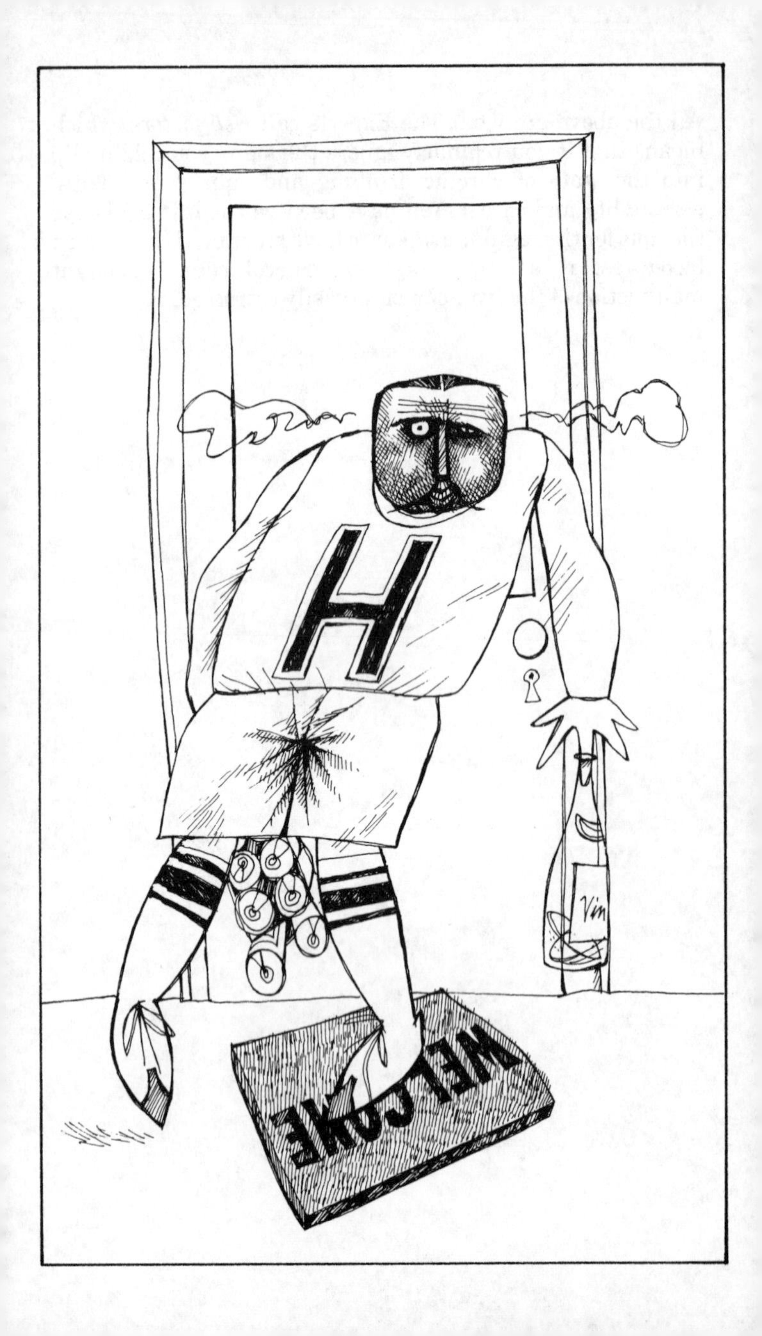
H
Vin
WELCOME

# A CHAPTER OF SUPERHOOLIGANS

# A CHAPTER OF SUPERHOOLIGANS

Superhooligans live life to the hilt, no doubt about it. They tour, travel the world, write brilliantly, paint, charm audiences and strangers, sell goods or themselves. They run homes, cook, look stylish, love and laugh a lot.

They work hard and play hard.

Their recipes for survival vary wildly; their approaches range from the practical to the philosophical, but they are all aware of the need to look after themselves in order to do their job to the best of their ability. And they do.

They are also very aware of the need to wind down crazily from time to time. And how they do!

Sometimes they push themselves to the brink, but they are capable of recognising danger signals, any threat to the core of their being.

All of them can laugh at their mistakes, put on a cloak of discipline, and get on with it.

Long may they all live.

And us too.

**Annie Ross**

*Jazz singer, actress*. Simultaneously appearing in *The Pirates of Penzance* (eight shows a week) and filming in *Superman III* during the day.

'Tomorrow starts when I finish the show. I go straight home, take the bread for the morning toast out of the freezer, lay out the megadose vitamins I have sent over from the States, turn the video on in the bedroom and settle down with a nice large vodka and tonic. That is the first drink of the day. I love scotch, but it's bad for the voice and I never drink before the show.

In the morning I take a gram of vitamin C, vitamin E 1000 IU, Vitamin B-Stress and Pharmaton, a ginseng plus vitamin E and pollen combination. I wash the lot down with a glass of grapefruit juice and feel I've done myself a good turn. It may be psychological, but it works for me. Three prunes to clear the system, some porridge for the fibre and I'm ready for the car at 6.30 a.m. Midday I have a steak in the canteen for protein, and when the filming is done I crash out in the car on the way to the theatre. Then I have to psyche myself up saying energy, energy, and it works so well that by the end of the show I'm on an adrenalin high again. I have the first cigarette of the day during the interval and sip herbal tea — Red Zinger (don't you love the name?) with honey.

If I'm not filming I go out to play with friends after the show, and if the evening has been too much fun I wash the vitamins down with Coca-Cola in the morning. When I'm working I don't eat dairy produce because it creates mucus; but I love cooking so long as I can get to the shops. I'll do a rataouille or a chicken soup with lots of leeks and carrots and onions. I'll eat anything; boiled necks of chicken, sucking the marrows out, or brains in butter when I can, I'll even eat the bones of tinned salmon — love scrunching them in my teeth.

That's when I'm working. When I'm not working, things can get a bit different. They say you should drink a lot of water at night after a good skinful. But how do you reach the tap from the floor?'

**John Gold**

*Owner of London's most consistently successful nightclub 'Tramp'*. His shrewd and genial eye has seen the likes of George Best, John Conteh, Ringo Starr and Bjorn Borg out celebrating a victory or two — a job that requires his fullest attention till the early hours of six mornings a week.

'During my working life I find it rather difficult to be a Hooligan myself; I have too many on most nights to look after.

However, holidays are another matter. After a very heavy boozy night an ice-cold lager (Foster's) first thing in the morning clears most of the collywobbles. After recovering slightly, my stomach is ready for an evening meal; my choice is normally a cream soup (to help drown the alcoholic leprechauns) followed by a plain grilled sole (sauce is a no-no).

I'm afraid I'm not very good on the health front, except mundane matters like not taking sugar, salt or butter, and I eat very little red meat. When I remember, I take an American multivitamin pill, the name of which I don't know because my dog licked the label off. He looks great on it, but I'm still struggling.'

**Janet Street-Porter**

*Journalist, author, and star of London Weekend Television.* She runs two homes, one in Yorkshire the other in Limehouse, and is married to Frank Cvitanovich, the television film director.

'I take Oil of Evening Primrose and multivitamin pills every day. If I feel particularly lousy, I also take Korean ginseng pills to pull me round. If I have a headache in the morning I take homeopathic pills for it but they don't work if you drink. If they haven't done their job by lunchtime I move on to something stronger like the hair of the dog.

Frank makes the most wonderful recovery breakfast — perfect scrambled eggs. For the evenings when we both feel absolutely terrible and exhausted, I have a marvellous gadget in the store cupboard — an electric pasta machine. All you need is eggs and strong white flour; pasta is quick to make and cooks in less than five minutes. Really comforting. I don't eat meat if I don't feel good, just add vegetable sauces or cream to the pasta.

The other thing I keep is cans of beer in the fridge — great for the dehydration. I won't buy mineral water, it's a waste of my money; but I drink loads of tap water with lemon, and I start the day with hot water with a slice of lemon too. I also drink lots of herbal tea without milk, which I find very refreshing and soothing.'

**Francis Bacon**

*Britain's foremost painter.* Somewhere in his seventies and still going strong, he disappears for weeks when he is working, but has been known to consume vast quantities of champagne during the run-up and wind-down periods.

'I have never found any panacea for a hangover. I don't think one exists apart from suicide.'

**Dai Llewllyn**

*Darling of the gossip columnists, launcher-of-nightclubs extraordinaire.*

'I used to keep fit jogging between girlfriends, pretending I was taking the dog for a run; but Vanessa (now my wife) noticed that the dog was getting fatter as I got thinner at around the same time somebody mentioned seeing him locked in the car all the time.

So now I don't get as much exercise, but luckily I have natural good health. I certainly drink a lot more than many of my friends who have fallen by the wayside. I don't believe in vitamins except for recuperating from an illness; the human body is a marvellous thing and has amazing powers of recovery.

I eat well, proper meals, not picking at bits and pieces. I eat whatever I feel like, usually vast quantities of meat, anything from venison to veal. And I do believe in the importance of potatoes for anyone who drinks; they contain vitamin C and potassium. I often have a cold potato, a small slice of low-fat cheese and half a tomato for breakfast. Just enough to support the champagne and orange juice until I get bored with the orange juice.

When I have been on a particularly hazardous few days, I do notice a slight ache in the kidneys which I deal with by drinking gallons of Perrier or San Pellegrino. I also always drink mineral water with my first course. I almost never drink in the afternoons, but then the evenings invariably go on to four in the morning, so the champagne does get rather a lengthy innings.'

**Jilly Johnson**

*Top model.* Her beautiful body is known to millions — though few will recall her name.

'On the days when I look in the mirror and see this near-geriatric delinquent I take two grams of effervescent vitamin C and while these are dissolving I run the bath with cold water.

When the vitamin C is ready I use it to knock back a couple of high-potency vitamin B pills, and then I kneel by the bath and plunge my head in right up to my shoulders. Honestly, you don't know what's hit you — but within minutes the Eyedew is in, the hair wrapped up, clothes on and you are out of the door and on your way to work. There isn't time for a hangover.

For the rest I'm not very good on the health bit; I like junk food, and could live on scrambled eggs and frozen vegetables. But when I'm not working too hard I do make nice meals with fresh meat and vegetables.'

**George Melly**

*Blues singer, writer, critic, expert on surrealist art.* On the road most of the year, and annually resident at Ronnie Scott's grotto at Christmas.

'I have to admit that I have absolutely nothing to do with vitamins. The rest of the band (John Chilton and the Feetwarmers) fill themselves with pills till they rattle, but I have never voluntarily bought a healthful jar of medicaments. Mind you, I drink a great deal less than I did and I have foresworn spirits altogether. I had to. Too many quite unalluring incidents. When strong drink starts killing off all the other pleasures in life it is time to give it up. I have been extremely lucky in being able to compromise, so now I drink wine or sherry and still manage to get a little buzz.

I have a Campari and soda in the morning. It gives a slight sense of taking medicine and cleans the throat; the bitter taste has the added attraction of making one feel virtuous, (always a good start to a day) while restoring a certain sense of wellbeing. A straight swig from a bottle of Angostura bitters can also be very reviving.

I have always been a great eater; to give up food for drink is really a bad step. My food tastes swing from wildly expensive meals in Wheeler's to black pudding and bacon at a café round the corner — but eat I must.'

**Susie Elliott**

*American wife of actor Denholm Elliott.* Open-house hostess to friends, colleagues, stars and hopefuls, her house is a 24-hour business with the 'phone ringing from across several continents at all kinds of unsociable hours.

'The only cure I know for living it up too well and too long is my Water Diet. It is quite drastic-sounding, takes a great deal of will-power (and ego), but it is 99 per cent cheaper than a health farm. You take nothing but mineral water for somewhere between 24 and 48 hours.

I buy eight litres of Evian Water, but it can be any mineral water, never tap water. I always begin the regimen around 6 p.m. as this means you can sleep through most of the first part. You must drink at least two litres every 12 hours. I always take a laxative at the start because the whole point of the operation is to get rid of the toxics in the body, and this speeds up the process. I usually lose about six pounds in the first 48 hours, but that is just an incidental plus factor. I do it to feel better and to look better.

Obviously you have to plan this marathon for times when you have no dates to play, because trying to socialise and keep to the diet is not just torture — it's impossible.

Otherwise I take natural Vitamin B12, Becosym B complex and one gram vitamin C daily.

Back off the wagon and suffering with day-after pains as far as I am concerned there is nothing to beat the iced-cold-bottle-of-champagne and scrambled-eggs-on-toast cure. Sets you up nicely for the evening games to come.'

**Ian Wooldridge**

*Sportswriter of the Year 1982*. His job involves travelling thousands of miles a year interviewing the Superstars of Fitness, meeting cronies in desperate need of gossip replenishment, and actually getting words on to paper.

'Sports johnnies tend to travel between 100,000 and 150,000 miles in a good expense-account-paid year. Thus to the usual hangover add what is often known as jet-lag.

Recipe: London-Sydney. Four large dry martinis as soon as possible on take-off. Sleep to Bombay. Four large dry Martinis out of Bombay. Sleep to Singapore. Four large dry Martinis out of Singapore. Sleep to Sydney.

Get off 'plane and immediately play 18 holes of golf. Don't eat at all. This may sound like bullshit, but it works. It's the eating that makes you feel like a ton of angora wool.

Golden rule for desperate hangover. Don't speak to anyone. Speaking guarantees divorce, sack, lost contracts. If hangover lasts beyond 4 p.m. sign the pledge immediately. If vastly improved by midday, go straight to bar for half-bottle claret with steak tartare to restore confidence in survival and give instant strength. All vitamins useless. Never read Christmas features on how to avoid hangovers since they are written by puritans who've never had a proper one.

Take taxis when drinking because it takes too long to park near the next good bar or hotel.

Never jog.

Never accept invitations from people who ban smoking in their homes; walk out immediately if caught by surprise and someone objects. Do everything possible to dissuade kids from smoking on the grounds that if they don't they will be able to buy a Lear Jet at 26.

Final thought: abstinence is the prerogative of the dead.'

**Jilly Cooper**

*Journalist, best-selling author.* The only blonde who has managed to be lusted after by half the world and still appear human to the other half.

'Living and drinking and working the way Leo (my husband) and I do, we certainly need all the help we can get. I must say I find one of the best cures for a hangover is fresh air, so I usually get up, plug myself with vitamin C and stagger out on to the Common with the dogs, trying to breathe in great gasps of oxygen. If I nearly get run over when crossing the road, I know it's bad.

That's my tale of the dogs; I never take the hair, as I think the hangover only comes back much worse later.

When I was in Australia doing a really gruelling promotion tour, the publicity girl handed me a tube of vitamin A and B compound pills that were absolutely incredible. On the packet it said they were for pregnancy, liver complaints and extreme alcoholism, but they worked wonders. They are made by Roche of Switzerland. One of the most fatal things to order for lunch when you've been on the booze is Dover Sole. Invariably it seems like a frightfully good idea because it is fish (good for you) and plain. Then greed sets in and you accept a great gobbet of tartare sauce and by the time you've got to the coffee stage you feel like throwing up. It's the fat in the fish and the sauce.

I always try to eat masses of oranges, but I am also always battling with diet versus drink. Drink is fatal; you lose all self-control over food, and in any case have to pack it in the next day to combat the alcohol.

'What is invaluable is to stay sober enough to remember to take a couple of Alka-Seltzers at night, then you really can wake up without a hangover. The only thing is that I think I'm King of the World at that stage, so I'm quite sure I *won't* have a hangover; then the thing creeps up and mercilessly knocks me sideways in the morning.

The great cure is sleep; but living in a noisy house with dogs barking, children shrieking and husband yelling is not conducive to a lengthy lie-in. A monastery can often seem awfully seductive.'

**JAK**

*Political cartoonist of the London* New Standard, *judo expert.* He is in the office at 7.30 every morning facing the loneliest job of all — a piece of blank paper that must be filled with a witty and topical cartoon by lunchtime.

'I get up at 5.45 a.m. and exercise in the bathroom, that is if I can stand up. If the hangover is too bad, I don't bother. I am into the fibre-diet way of health; at the beginning of each week I mix a huge container-full of dried fruits, nuts, bran, oats, the lot, so that each morning I can grab a portion, slurp milk on it, have a cup of hot tea and be ready for the car to collect me. Driving is a bit taboo this year.

If the hangover is monumental, I go into my water routine. I keep a magnum-sized champagne bottle in the office, fill it with iced water and drink the lot. Sometimes I drink peppermint tea instead, and sometimes I'll weaken and have a double fried-egg sandwich from the canteen around nine. If

Fig. 1

things are really bad around eleven, I'll collect Frank Dickens and we go to the pub for half of Guinness — which usually becomes a pint — and a couple of sausages with plenty of mustard.

Otherwise I go to Lamb's Squash Club in the Barbican and play with a pro for half an hour. That's just about all I can manage. It's the worst method of revival you can think of — real hell while you're doing it, all that sweat pouring out of you, but after a shower you do actually feel better.

I also try and keep fit by going to the gymnasium occasionally, where Len puts me through my paces. Mostly by the time I have finished work I am ready to accompany a few friends to lunch.

I need only five or six hours' sleep, but if I've been out on the town I may only get two. After a couple of those nights, after work I head for home and take Max the dog out for a run. Since he doesn't drink he sensibly comes half way with me, then waits for me to return so he can lead me home. And that's both of us finished for the day.

I've tried vitamins erratically, but never found them to make much difference. I really think keeping fit is the answer.'

**Ed Devereaux**

*Australian actor, scriptwriter.* He commutes between two continents, working in films, television and theatre, playing a lush in *Rocket to the Moon* in the West End. Recently he had major heart surgery, an event that forced him to give up smoking and take more soda with it.

'I have always lived by the advice my father gave me when I was a young man; if you want to live a long life, don't have anything to do with bad whisky or good women.

Apart from that I believe in eating a varied diet and plenty of it. I also take a gram of vitamin C daily, boosting the dosage in the winter, and I take vitamin B, Orovite, every day, which I wash down with the whisky.'

Fig. 2

**Wendy Richards**

*Comedy actress.* In the television series 'Are You Being Served?'. Lengthy provincial tours feature heavily in her life style as well as the opening of fêtes and supermarkets.

'I was doing summer season in Blackpool and my hotel was just across from an abbattoir. The reality of meat-eating hit me there and then, and I have been a vegetarian ever since. That's when I became interested in vitamins. I eat masses of fresh fruit and vegetables, so I don't need extra vitamin C; but I do take the whole vitamin B complex, vitamin E for my skin, and cod-liver oil capsules. Then I found some amazing pills called Efamol, which contain Oil of Evening Primose. I took them for my PMT but, amazingly, I haven't had a hangover since I started on them.

I deal with any dehydration by drinking mineral water until opening time — then there is nothing like a bottle of pink champagne to revive the flagging spirit.'

**Eddie Chapman**

*Writer, super safe-breaker and super spy.* The only British agent to win the Iron Cross. He now runs a health farm, Shenley Lodge in Hertfordshire, with his wife Betty.

'A day should start with style. A breakfast of smoked Irish bacon, two English fried eggs, some button mushrooms, two chipolatas, some wholemeal toast spread with Dutch butter, all beautifully laid out on a tray. This should be served to you in bed.

When the door has closed, the sight of it will provoke a strong desire to vomit. Go to the French windows and chuck the whole bloody lot out on to the lawn. This will bring your wife, guests and staff rushing to the room, where an almighty row will break out. This will get the adrenalin pumping in everyone — the perfect cure for a hangover.

A gentle shower with scented soap, then off to a Seventh-Day-Adventist masseur; they are so repressed, they will punish you if you make a sound. Thus all guilt for any nefarious behaviour is assuaged.

You are then ready to continue the day with a half-bottle of Dom Perignon and a freshly-squeezed peach mixed together and served in a silver goblet; 'Angel's Kiss' it is called. It has always seemed to me that in order to enjoy feeling fit you have to have been a sinner.'

**Barbara Griggs**

*Journalist, author, and expert on herbal remedies.* She is married to a Dutch journalist, Henri van der Zee, and they have co-authored several historical biographies.

'You could label us Hooligan and Counterhooligan, because I cannot drink as well as Henri. I never touch spirits, they make me quarrelsome or tearful; but we are both pretty avid health freaks.

We both take three grams of vitamin C if we have been out late at night, and in the morning we have brewers' yeast tablets, another gram of vitamin C, a strong vitamin E, 1000 IU and vitamin B12. We avoid coffee like the plague, also cheap plonk; that really does hit the liver. Earl Grey tea is soothing, as is a lemon squeezed into a glass of warm water; that is one of the finest tonics you can give the liver.

There is a new herbal remedy on the market, Oil of Evening Primose. Four to six capsules taken at night helps prevent a hangover. I have even tried them when I've woken up feeling cloudy and horrible and they have made the birds sing again.

Another good trick for the morning, the days when your very eyes are dehydrated and your lids feel as if they are made of sandpaper, is to keep a bottle of witch hazel in the fridge. Soak a couple of pads of cotton wool in it and lie down for a few minutes with them over your eyes; you soon feel full of sparkle. Good, too, if an evening has ended in tears. Failing witch hazel, used tea bags, chilled in the fridge, work wonders. A couple of times a week we take seaweed pills, zinc, and dolomite for the calcium. I have every intention of keeping my teeth to a ripe old age.

For facing the world outside there is nothing like a cold Heineken straight from the fridge. It's a sort of hair from a friendly dog.

If we have to face a professional lunch, we aim to keep the food simple. Melon, grilled sole or lamb cutlets. Never refuse wine — it makes the host uncomfortable — but always ask for some mineral water as well. That way you can take the occasional sip of the wine but swig the water greedily. Nobody will really be noticing.'

**Freddie Jones**

*A great British actor.* The star of numerous West End productions and of a new Fellini film.

'There are those who can take Life neat — as for myself I find it palatable only when diluted by roughly eight black-and-tans or tweleve large scotches *per diem*.

I gained my philosophy from a discussion with two memorable Hindus. I was complaining bitterly about a friend's wanton cruelty towards me, when they informed me that, surely, we must love one another for our weaknesses, not our strengths. And it is true; I cannot easily trust a person who neither drinks nor smokes. This is palpably non-viable as a criterion but I prefer to seek out my fellows in smoky bars and join in an orgy of laughter (and therefore tears), of improvisation, spontaneity, memories and shared notes on Life and Death. They, too, have looked at the Human Condition somewhere in pubescene, and have declined to join; they wish to be Country or Honorary Members only.

So my main source of food is Guinness, from which I receive all the vitamins I need; and as I can't drink after I have eaten I am inclined to take what little food I eat at very odd hours. Sometimes I feel I owe it to myself to do more and buy a huge bottle of super-vitamins — only to discover them on the shelf years later. I will probably have taken three.

I have to err on the side of right when working, more because the drink is heavy and I like to feel physically light, but that does not preclude pleasures after working hours. So it follows that a great deal of my life has been wonderfully enriched by people hooked on a life-long game of Russian roulette. And there have been tragic losses. And there have been priceless gains. Cheers!'

**Jeffrey Bernard**

*Humorist, author of 'Low Life' in* The Spectator, *co-author of* High Life, Low Life. The only man ever heard to apologise to the landlord of his local for being five minutes late.

'The most important rule that drinkers should observe above all others is that it is essential to be drunk all the time. Sobriety causes hangovers, tremors and, in serious cases, even delirium tremens. Sobriety apart, the drinker should avoid any form of exercise. Never walk to a pub. Always take a taxi. Walking can effectively speed up the circulation, but it's far safer to sit on a bar stool and allow whisky to do just that. There's a lot of talk these days about jogging to keep fit — but fit for what? Any violent physical movement outside a pub or bar is a potential killer, and the drinker should restrict his exercise to putting his hand in his pocket or her handbag and to writing out the occasional cheque.

Food is essential, but valuable drinking money shouldn't be wasted on particularly good food. Nursery food keeps the doctors at bay and soothes the angry liver. Minced meat and mashed potatoes should be taken twice a day. For a stomach lining I can recommend a banana and a half-pint of milk mixed in a blender shortly before opening time. On retiring to the floor at night the drinker should consume one or two pints of water if he or she can find the tap.

But however dedicated you may be to drinking, there are drinks to be avoided. This is bad news, I know, but aperitifs contain so many congeners of alcohol that they are almost poisonous. Of the spirits, brandy contains the most congeners and vodka the fewest. I have vodka coming out of my ears and yet my hearing is perfect; in fact, I can hear the bolt on a pub door sliding back at 11 a.m. from 500 yards.

Although it is unprofessional and bad-mannered to refuse a drink, the boozer should try to restrict himself to one double every twenty minutes. It sounds mean, but you can actually get through 36 doubles or just over two bottles a working day. And, speaking of work, like exercise it should be avoided. Drinking is no less than a career, and as such needs dedication.

As for hangovers resulting from accidentally being parted from the bottle for too long, a word about Bloody Marys. A slice of lemon is meaningless. The Bloody Mary requires the juice of one lime. Upset stomachs respond well to Crème de Menthe — the base of most hangover drinks — and it also speeds up the journey to euphoria.

It is a fact of life that the good days are the exception and not the rule. Generally speaking, Life is a bowl of shit and not of cherries. By staying drunk for most of the time you will find Life slipping quietly past without having to notice just how awful it is.'

**Shirley Young**

*Leading fashion-consultant, public relations*. Her job extends well outside office hours; socialising with clients, soothing ruffled designers' nerves, dealing with excitable models, photographers and travel.

'Unfortunately I can't drink as much as I'd like to — certainly not as much as the company I keep — because I suffer from migraine if I do. But because I am in a youth-orientated job I bombard myself with vitamins, take Migril if I am going out on a toot or travelling, and drink masses of Malvern Water.

I try to make sure the food we eat at home is fresh, with plenty of meat, vegetables and fruit, and only wholemeal bread.

The two best aids to healthy looks are still free. A long bracing walk in the country, especially in the rain, is very refreshing after a hard day and a long drive and wonderful for the skin. The other one is sleep. I still believe in the old adage that the hours of sleep before midnight are the youth hours, so when I'm not working late I try to get to bed at 10 p.m.; with a day that starts at 6 a.m. I have no difficulty sleeping.'

**Barbara Cartland**
*Prolific novelist and chief champion of the value of vitamins.* She has taken her own medicine for years, and her energy is irrefutable evidence of their value. She travels thousands of miles yearly, socialises with verve, and writes every day. Her daily intake of vitamins is legendary but she adds this advice for the hard-working traveller.

'I recommend something which I find quite fantastic for jet-lag. I take four Panax Ginseng before leaving, and then two every four hours during the flight. I tell all my friends to do the same, and they have found it a tremendous help.'

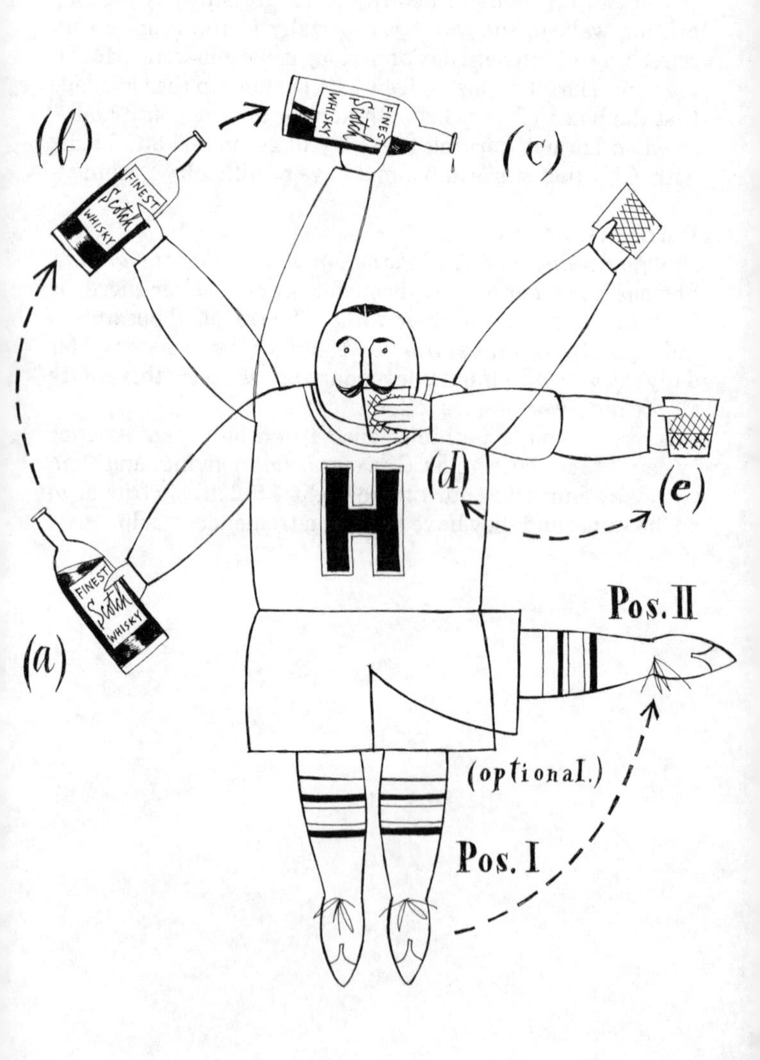
(b)
FINEST
Scotch
WHISKY
(c)
(d)
(e)
(a)
Pos. II
(optional.)
Pos. I

# PRAISE BE . . .

# PRAISE BE . . .

So now all Hooligans give Praise — to whoever out there in uncharted history discovered alcohol, and Thanks — to Mother Nature for providing the nourishment for us to live long enough to enjoy it.

As I have pointed out, vitamins are not as expensive as they first appear but, knowing the character of Hooligans, you will probably all rush out and buy the lot. As you know, Hooligans seldom do things by halves.

So a delicate word in your ear as you commence this onslaught of health. Sometimes the sudden rush of vitamins to the body can disturb what has become a lazy piece of mechanism, and they can shift the subtle balance of internal chemistries. This means you will fart like a good 'un during the first few days. Nothing wrong with that. The body — dear, phenomenal thing that it is, will soon adapt — particularly if your new-found sense of wellbeing drives you towards food.

Even so, it is only fair to warn you that Oystertone can, at first, produce especially treacherous results. Never risk a sneaky one, however urgent the tension, in public. It will hang around the company like an unloved mongrel dog. This,

BEANZ
BAKED
BEANS

too, will pass (the state, I mean); taking Oystertone after a fibre-type breakfast helps considerably.

Another characteristic of the Hooligan is to run out of enthusiasm for new ventures quite quickly, so there will be times when the vitamins sit neglected on the shelf. Do not worry; their effectiveness lasts for at least a couple of years so long as they are not kept near sunlight.

Some people protest that they cannot take vitamins because swallowing pills makes them gag. There are ways and means of dealing with this problem. You tilt your head right back and open your throat as if you were receiving the first drink after Lent. Using effervescent vitamin C to wash pills down helps. Alternatively, you can use your favourite tipple — bet you don't gag on that.

Do, occasionally, take time off to listen to your body. If it actually doesn't fancy a drink, don't force it. Short of the holocaust, the pub will still be there in the morning. Become, as a friend of mine calls it, a Secret Abstainer — much healthier than becoming a Secret Imbiber.

For those who fancy a really personalised chart for health, there is such a thing as hair analysis. This does not require the painful plucking of hair from the roots — just two or three teaspoonsful from the nape of the neck (balding men may breathe a sigh of relief here) so that the hair to be analysed is reasonably new. The hair is sent to the University of Aston in Birmingham for deficiency detection, and you will receive advice accordingly. The cost of the analysis is approximately that of two bottles of the hard stuff. Anyone wanting details of this service should send the usual stamped addressed envelope to Diet-Mart (HA), Unit 18, Goldsworth Park Trading Estate, Woking, Surrey GU21 3BJ.

I hope I have convinced you of the pleasures of being a Healthy Hooligan, and that the information contained in this book will be equally useful after any lapses. May the Blessings of Bacchus be with you for ever. Cheers!